How to quit

Julian Kirkman-Page
(With a foreword by Dan Jones)

After 40 years of drinking and ending up a total mess with type 2 diabetes, high blood pressure, gout and even a frighteningly short-term outlook on life, one day in 2012 I decided to quit alcohol forever. Without resorting to drugs, rehab or any outside help I've never touched a drop since, and have never been so wonderfully healthy or happy in my life. This comprehensive guide takes you through how I did it and what a phenomenal difference it has made to me, so you can enjoy the same!

Mallard Publishing

It works, it's easy, it's unique and most especially, it's great FUN!

Discussion

A proven methodology

Day by Day advice

Hilarious tales

Includes a self-hypnosis session to download

Dedicated to my darling wife Lolly,

for putting up with everything

Contents

Who am I?

You could say I have 'been there and done that'. If I was to create a jigsaw puzzle to depict my life, it would a 3D 1,000 piece version and far from complete. I have worked in a shop, been a City businessman, owned my own company, been a science teacher and even managed a tobacco farm. I have known success and failure and even watched my card being swallowed by the bank machine as I waved goodbye to my last few pounds (mind you despite this I still managed to find enough pennies to buy a bottle of wine and some fags!) I have been sacked and I have sacked people, I have travelled far and wide and seen a lot of what's good and bad in the World, I have even had a gun held to my head. I have known sublime happiness and deep despair. I have had marriages and divorces, been a single parent, seen the miracle of my two daughters brought into the World, and known the sorrow of saying goodbye to parents and both brothers. I have even watched my mother and elder brother drink themselves to death. I am a scientist but I embrace all the World's religions equally and have my own deep philosophy on life. But if one piece of the jigsaw puts all the rest into perspective, and will help me complete a picture I would be happy to frame and be proud of, it is being able to finally say:

'I don't drink!'

Foreword by Dan Jones, founder of 'The Sussex Hypnotherapy Centre'

It is not often a book comes along that offers the reader exactly what they are looking for. This book does just that.

As a therapist I have worked with people that want to stop drinking alcohol for over 20 years, and in all those years I have yet to find a book that I can recommend to my clients. This book is the exception. It isn't written by a therapist, it isn't full of research and jargon, and it isn't too long.

This book gets to the point; it gives a clear and easy to follow 'no nonsense' approach. It is full of real life examples from an author that has 'been there and done that'.

In 'I Don't Drink!' Julian Kirkman-Page shares his insights on how he came up with an effective way of quitting drinking, and staying stopped. His process fits with the way I do therapy that I've written about on many occasions in my educational books for therapists, focusing on the future, focusing on being positive and placing most of your focus on what you will gain, rather than obsessing about the problem or the 'why'. I have spent years learning about how to treat people that want to quit drinking, and most of this learning has actually come from clients and what they tell me what works for them rather than what I have learnt from textbooks and training courses. Julian's book 'I Don't Drink!' is a prime example of how a person that has had a problem can teach more about how to treat that problem than any textbook.

My therapeutic philosophy is that the person with the problem knows more than anyone else what they need to do in order to overcome their problem, they just don't always realise they know this. That is where the role of a therapist comes in. A therapist can act as a guide for the client, helping them find their way. The client has the map, and the therapist has the torch.

I met Julian at a local group for authors called Chindi (Chichester Independent Authors) where he spoke about the book he had written called 'The 7:52 To London Bridge'. This book is an autobiographical collection of tales of adventure and misadventure. When I read the book I noticed there was a theme that weaved through most of the tales. It was an enjoyable and humorous and at times a moving read, but it was also clear that Julian spent a lot of time drinking to excess, in fact from reading his book it seemed much of his life revolved around alcohol.

This surprised me, because when I met Julian at the first Chindi meeting I attended which was taking place in a bar in Chichester and he was asked what he wanted to drink his reply was 'I Don't Drink'. After I had read Julian's first book and I noticed the Julian in the book seemed to be a heavy drinker, whereas the Julian I know tells everyone 'I Don't Drink' I asked about this difference. The Julian I know regularly goes swimming, and can comfortably swim a mile, he is often out to sea kayaking or scuba diving, or just enjoying the sea, he is very active and to me he looks very fit, healthy, always smiling, and full of life, he looks much younger than his true age, and none of this fits with what I would expect of the Julian in his book.

Julian told me that he used to drink heavily and had many health problems; including gout, high blood pressure, was close to being diagnosed with diabetes, was overweight, and that his mother and brother both passed away due to alcohol but that he was now writing this book.

The difference between the person Julian described to me and the person Julian is now is incredible. I wanted to know how he did it, was it something I could teach to my clients, how can others do as Julian did and say 'I Don't Drink'?

The answer to these questions is 'yes', it is something I can teach to my clients, and others can do as Julian has done.

In this book, Julian shares an honest and frank description of how alcohol has featured in his life, in his family's life and the impact alcohol has had in the past. You will hear how thinking about all the fun you have had drinking can help you to stay stopped now. There are tales from both sides of the drinking coin, stories about drunken fun Julian has had, as well as tales about the negative impact of drinking.

If you are going to be reading this because you want to become a person that can say 'I Don't Drink' then this book is definitely for you.

Dan Jones

Founder of 'The Sussex Hypnotherapy Centre'

Best-Selling Author of 'Hypnotherapy' and 'Advanced Ericksonian Hypnotherapy Scripts'

Chichester, West Sussex, UK

November 2014

Introduction

Congratulations, the very act of opening this book means you have a strong desire to say goodbye to alcohol once and for all and become someone who can proudly say 'I don't drink!'

You will have thought about giving up drinking before, perhaps you have even given it a go but you need that extra push, that extra drive to help you succeed once and for all. Hopefully this book will be that final motivation that you need.

Most importantly, I hope I can help you become someone who openly says 'I don't drink' without secretly wishing you still did drink; without looking with envy at the delicious looking glass of wine, beer or spirit in the hand of the person you are talking to, but instead with an inner self-satisfied 'been there done that' feeling coupled with the confidence that you won't be going there again, thank-you.

I don't set out to preach in this book why you should stop drinking, nor do I offer sound medical advice tailored to your specific needs, only **you** know why you want to or must stop drinking. Instead, what I do is tell you how one day in my mid-fifties I finally decided to never drink again, how I have managed to never have a drink since that day, how it is only at the rarest of times I get a flash-back and think a drink would be nice and even then only for a second. How I have even got to the stage where the very thought of drinking anything alcoholic can make me physically feel all the unpleasant after-affects, and why I would never consider winding back the clock to my pre 'I don't drink' days. And believe me when I say that if I can do it so can you, as you will discover. You will read more about me in the stories in this book and all will become crystal clear.

Let me start by briefly telling you what I have achieved so far:-

- By the time this book is published I will have been a non-drinker for two years. For someone who spent their adult life (and much of their teenage years) drinking too much, that is a huge achievement in itself.
- I have managed to give up drink without having to resort to the use of drugs or stimulants of any kind and without any medical help.
- I have got rid of my high blood pressure and no longer need to take any tablets.
- I have got rid of my high cholesterol and no longer need to take any tablets.

- I have completely got rid of gout and all the crippling pain and lingering disability that comes with it.
- The psoriasis I had since I was a child has disappeared.
- Not that I was particularly overweight, but without trying I have lost two stone (28 pounds / 13 kilos) in weight, and I am now firmly in the normal BMI range for my age and build.
- I have saved a huge amount of money.
- I have never felt so fit or been so active, even from when I was a child.
- My days are now so full and productive and I have never achieved so much in such a short a space of time.
- I feel at least ten years younger, and am told I look a lot younger as well (although modesty makes me reluctant to admit to this), and people say I have a far brighter 'twinkle in my eye'.
- I have a totally different outlook on life and expect to live to a ripe old age, no longer being of the opinion that purely living until retirement age was some sort of success and could be considered a 'good innings'.
- Most importantly, I have never felt so happy and content and have made those close to me much happier by being a nicer person to live with and be around.

Oh and by the way;

In 2011 I was told by my doctor I had type 2 diabetes but that if I lost weight and changed my lifestyle the disease might not develop. I lost a little weight and went for my six monthly check-ups but nothing much happened. Then I gave up alcohol:

My type 2 diabetes has gone!

The really great thing is that most of the above I achieved within just a few weeks of giving up drink. It really doesn't take long for the benefits to take hold, and this is just a short summary, it doesn't include the healthier lifestyle I now enjoy or the internal improvements to my body that can't be seen directly such as my brand new healthy liver!

Something else has become apparent and very noticeable now I have managed nearly two years of no drinking. In writing down for this book some of my experiences at key events such as weddings and on major holidays, I realise how much more freedom I have now that I don't drink. I can clearly see just how much drink used to dictate my life without my even being consciously aware of it, to what a great extent my day would be planned around drink, how many things I was missing out on because drink was getting in the way, or I was simply not enjoying to the full because drink (or more to the point the lack of having the drink I thought I needed) was causing so much stress and anxiety.

So please read on and see how to use this book, learn about my own methodology that has and continues to work so well for me; have a lot of fun long the way, and hopefully join me in also being proud to enjoy saying:

'I don't drink!'

Why is my book different?

This book is different from other material you will have either bought, been given or found on the net.

First of all it is not written by an academic. It is written by me, someone who has been through what you are going to experience. Someone who was a big drinker for more than forty years and as you will learn, even reluctantly admits to having been an alcoholic. Someone who no longer drinks. Someone who despite the constant temptation and no matter what life throws at me, will never drink again.

Secondly, instead of just pages of text to wade through once and then put to one side, I provide you with a day to day list of things to do, things to think about and try not to think about, and a proven methodology that worked for and continues to work for me. So this is very much a working book you can keep with you and turn to as you experience challenges I have already coped with, perhaps for guidance, perhaps just for support, but also just to know you are not the only one.

Thirdly, everything in this book is true. It is not hearsay or gleaned by some researcher based on a series of surveys or interviews, but all down to my own first-hand experience.

It is an amusing book because giving up drink is actually enjoyable!

Although at this stage you will find it hard to imagine and believe, I really do enjoy and get immense pleasure from not drinking. But I also enjoy looking back on having been a drinker to laugh at the fun times I have had, and to delight at the misery I have experienced that I will never have to go through again. It is almost like imagining it happened to someone else. But I don't want to try and change my past (you can't anyway), so I don't harp on about negative things I did and wish they had never happened. Instead by way of promoting a 'been there, done that' attitude I include what I hope you will agree are some of my very funny and true stories involving drink! And part of my methodology is to encourage you to write down or at least think about some of your own.

Been there – done that!

I promote a forward thinking and completely positive

approach to enjoying your new life as a non-drinker. I do not include all the ambiguous medical reasons not to drink (there is always a counter argument if you want one), instead as we go through the book I highlight what has happened and what is happening to me from a health and lifestyle perspective, most of which I put down to conquering alcohol. You can google all the medical, philosophical, psychological and physiological reasons not to drink (and the converse) for yourself, there are thousands of pages on the subject. I expect however you will become confused, bored or simply use the whole exercise as an excuse to put off the big day. Myself, I never bothered with any of it. I have enough common sense to know that alcohol is bad for you, and now I have the proof positive. Being told by someone I know, that someone they know, met someone who has an uncle who knows someone who lived to be ninety three, who never had an ill day in their life and drank like a trooper is just a massive red herring.

I would wish you good luck, but you won't need it. You already have all you require, it's called self-will and a determination to succeed; having chosen to read this book is firm evidence of that.

So have fun giving up drink and welcome to a whole new life

How to use this book

Once you have scanned the book to see how it hangs together and read through the few introductory chapters, spend some time going through the essential discussion chapters. Based on my own true responses they will help you decide things like:-

- Am I an alcoholic?
- Why am I giving up drink?
- When should I start to be a non-drinker?
- What essential things do I need to do and to plan?
- What do I tell other people and when?
- What should I expect to feel?
- What else might I have to give up?

Then when you are ready, find the page that simply shows the big **start button** and it's time to swallow hard and say 'I don't drink'.

The chapters following **start** are like diary pages and should help you as you go through the next few days and weeks, hopefully acting as reminders, pointers, providing clues as to what you can expect and offering encouragement.

The comical stories that are interwoven throughout the book are there to help with this and to encourage you to create your own stories, either in your head, in writing, in picture form or maybe even recorded so you can play them back to yourself when you feel the need. They form a fundamental part of my **methodology.**

There are more of these stories to be found on my website which you can either read on-line or download for free:

www.idontdrink.net

Hopefully once you have begun your new journey you will never need to go back to the start again, but if you do waver, there is further help immediately to hand.

Since giving up drink I have met and started working with Dan Jones who kindly wrote the foreword to this book for me. Dan is an expert at using hypnosis techniques to help people with addictions especially alcohol, and he has put together a short but effective session to accompany this book. Hopefully following my methodology will be more than enough to get you to where you also say 'I don't drink!', but if you would like additional support, the session can be accessed by following the special link at the back of this book.

Finally I would welcome your feedback so please join my blog.

Now Read On

Why did I write this book and for whom?

I decided to write this book because I am so delighted with my new life I thought it only fair to share the experience with **you**. To give you the same opportunity to be the person you know you really want to be.

Since I gave up drink a great many people I come into contact with have asked me how I have managed to give up drink, and most of them want to do the same but don't know where to start or need an extra incentive. I am no therapist and I certainly don't want to spend the rest of my working life running courses or competing with the many worthy organisations that offer help and counselling to drinkers. However, I do want to help where I can and this book is my way of doing that. If it helps you, and you become that new person as a result of finding a spark within these pages then everyone wins.

It is worth stating that this book is firmly aimed at the individual who has made the decision they want to give up drinking. But then if you are not convinced you have a problem, you won't even have got this far in the first place.

The book is also geared towards your partner should you have one. It will help your partner understand my approach to giving up drink and hopefully encourage them to allow you, the new non-drinker the space and time required to achieve this worthy goal. Any discouragement by way of negative waves (as Odd-ball would say in that great film Kelly's Heroes) will certainly not help.

With increasing publicity and awareness of the perils of drinking, reading this book may also help young people understand the need to limit their drinking or even decide not to drink in the first place. Certainly if I could turn the clock back and live the last thirty years without alcohol I would, but then hindsight is one reward for growing older. I don't think I would be much fitter than I have managed to get myself since I gave up, but there are so many things I could have done or done better if I had been completely sober. There are also some experiences as a result of drink I would definitely not want to have to go through again! Yes I generally had a lot of fun getting drunk, but I now know I can have just as much fun if not more without having a drink at all. I **CAN** be drunk without drinking!

But don't turn your back on drink!

By this I certainly don't mean have a drink, instead

what I mean is don't try and hide from drink. Avoiding pubs or social events where drink is going to be available, throwing away all the drink at home to the annoyance of those you live with etc. will only alienate you from your friends and delay you coming to terms with drink later on. You just have to rise above any temptation. I quickly found reliable substitutes in non-alcoholic beverages such green tea, lime and soda, drinking lots of water and having the occasional Italian coffee as a special treat, and finding that these new thirst quenching alternatives helped stop me wanting an alcoholic drink at all. I also bought some bottles of special cloudy lemonade and ginger beer expecting to need to treat myself regularly to something sweet, but I never did and they went past their sell by date unopened. I still meet with all my regular friends as always; I still do the same things with them, I even continue to meet my work colleagues in lunchtime wine bars, I just do a whole lot more things besides because I have so much more energy and more time on my hands as you will quickly realise. Oh, and I laugh just as much, if not more!

So what made me realise it was time to give up drink, and what led to me forming my methodology?

As a slight warning, this is the only sad tale in an otherwise hopefully fun-packed tome, and only included as a background to set the scene.

In 2012 I was still a drinker, but regardless of that had decided to fulfil a long-held ambition to write a book. This was to become an autobiographical comedy entitled 'The 7.52 to London Bridge' using the setting of my having spent thirty years commuting to London as a stage for a series of adventures and misadventures most of which coincidentally involved drink and most of which are quite hilarious (that's not me being vainglorious, I only feel justified saying that because it says that in some of the reviews received on amazon!)

The book is a series of 14 tales, and the first proper chapter I typed up is called 'The Mallard'. The Mallard is an amusing story set in the Leicester of my childhood with some great tales of the sort of mischief my elder brother and I got up to playing on the railway in the days of steam, and it culminates in me returning there with my family a few years ago, some fifty years later, to scatter my mother's ashes in the canal where she used to play when she was a child. In the story my mum's ashes are swiftly eaten by a squadron of mallards who appear as if from nowhere much to everyone's horror and subsequent amusement – but then that really is another story.

As I wrote that tale and looked through the photos I had taken of the occasion, it brought home the feelings I had on that day and tidings of what had happened since. My mum's death certificate stated alcoholic liver failure as the cause of her death. This had been a complete shock to me, and was brought home even more by seeing at the funeral her twin sister who was still as fit as a fiddle and also completely stunned to learn that her sister had been an alcoholic. I thought my mum just drank wine which is all I ever saw her drink, but it subsequently turned out she had been drinking bottles of vodka with my brother in the restaurant across the road every night for months if not years. She and my brother had both been hiding the fact from the rest of us (I only discovered the truth after my brother's death shortly after mum died).

Looking anew at the photographs of the ash scattering I could see my brother was already yellow skinned and looking about twenty years older than me instead of just five years. I remembered having to cope with him on the day as he became increasingly unruly as he drank more and as he started shouting, repeating himself and basically becoming a complete pain and a bore. I remembered feeling very much the responsible adult and worrying that he was going to do something to wreck the day and embarrass us all. I remembered going to the house where my mother and her sister had been brought up; asking the owner if we could look in the garden where they had watched the trains race past as little girls, and seeing the sceptical look on his face as he viewed my drink sodden and consequently suspicious looking brother. I remembered on the motorway back to London, passing my brother and his family crawling along in their car in the slow lane, hoping to avoid any chance of being stopped by the police and my brother being breathalysed. He died from drink a few months later, a complete and utter mess at the age of 56.

I saw him twice more before he died. Once when I visited him at a rehab clinic in Brighton I had encouraged him to put himself in to. That was another shock as he looked so bright yellow with jaundice, so incredibly old and so completely wasted. It was one of the private clinics where they lock you in for your own good and after a couple of weeks he did seem to be on the mend, but he was apparently 'rescued' from that clinic by some drinking 'friends' of his who were no doubt missing helping him spend his inheritance from our mother. The final time I saw him was just a few weeks later and in hospital, but he was already in a coma and not long for this World.

In writing the 'Mallard' and what was to become an amusing and nostalgic tale, I didn't write any of the nasty or sad bits in, I just concentrated on the fun parts, and the ash scattering really did have a funny ending, and I really did enjoy writing the story. But as I read and reread it as part of the editing process there was strong underlying and essential message coming through for myself.

That experience and that ash scattering day hadn't been all fun, there was a seriously sad side to it I had since closed my mind to. There was the fact my mother died a horrible unnecessary death and many years before her twin sister. There was the fact it was one of the last times I would ever see the brother I loved and who would never read my book full of happy stories about him and I as children, and see it become a success. There was the complete and senseless waste as well, and all the wonderful things that have happened since that my mum and brother were unable to share with me because they had killed themselves. When I think of all the times I still hear myself say 'wouldn't mum have loved this', or 'Paul would have laughed himself silly at this', it really can make me quite sad.

It must never happen to me and to mine. So I decided to enjoy remembering the fun and the drunken times and continue to write about them, but I must also remember the underlying message – I have 'been there and done that'. Enough is enough thank you.

As I carried on writing stories for that first book and committing to paper more and more drunken tales about my journeys:

It wouldn't be long before my own new journey would begin

Was I (are you) an alcoholic?

This is the really big question I am sure we all ask ourselves, and being an alcoholic is something I am sure we would rather not admit to. It also begs the equally big question, 'what is an alcoholic?' Is the chemical compound ethanol actually addictive or is it the drinking itself and the effects it gives that is addictive? In other words is your body craving that alcohol fix or is it your mind craving it?

I was certainly never diagnosed as an alcoholic. I knew I had a drink problem but I had visons of what an alcoholic looked like and how they behaved. Most tramps look like they are probably alcoholics especially if they are holding a can of special brew and shouting incoherent abuse, but then I have done that and I'm not a tramp so that doesn't help me place myself in the alcoholic category. Also, no doctor ever suggested I needed help even when I had been honest (or almost honest) about how much I was drinking, and I never ever considered needing to join any self-help group such as AA. In fact the only person who ever suggested I might be an alcoholic was my wife. But sometimes I would catch myself drinking purely for the sake of drinking, especially if I was drinking alone, and I would challenge myself and often ask myself the following simple set of questions to see if I could admit to myself I might be an alcoholic; how do you fare?

Question		Yes/no
1	Do I drink first thing in the morning	no
2	Do I physically feel I need a drink	no
3	Do I drink every day	no
4	Do I drink more than the recommended daily allowance	yes
5	Do I ever 'tank up'	yes
6	Do I ever plan my day around drink	yes

Oh dear, let's have a look at those questions and answers in more detail.

Question one

Answering the first question in the negative always gave me the comfort factor that I was not an alcoholic. I imagined an alcoholic would always behave this way and start the day with a drink. I would generally have my first drink at lunchtime if at work in the City, or mid-afternoon if it was a weekend. When I was teaching I didn't have a drink until late in the evening. So I can't have been an alcoholic.

Question two

I certainly know the feeling of 'needing a drink' but this has always been after a massive drinking session the night before, and I thought I knew that the best cure for that 'hung over' feeling was to have another drink. I have thankfully never 'consciously' got to the advanced stage where I don't feel I can cope without a drink or that my body will somehow pack in if I don't have a drink. I have also been in situations where I have been unable to have a drink for a day or two and I have been completely fine; my world hasn't fallen apart. So I can't have been an alcoholic.

Question three

I answered no to this but I did drink 'almost' every day. There would have to be a very good reason for me not to have a drink such as me being too ill to have a drink, or me being responsible for other people such as when helping out on a school trip. But I can't have been an alcoholic, surely?

Question four

If I was drinking, I would always greatly exceed the recommended daily allowance. This was not deliberate, it's just that the recommended allowance always seemed pitifully small, even to the extent it didn't seem even worth drinking. I did sort of set my own daily limit however and I discuss this much later on in the book because it's irrelevant at this stage.

Question five

If we were going out to the theatre for example, instead of having one glass of wine in the bar before the show, I would drink a whole two hours' worth as quickly as possible just to make sure I would be getting my 'daily allowance'. I would do the same if we were going to someone's house, even for drinks! I would assume they would either be mean with the drink or I knew I would be embarrassed if seen to be drinking too much, so I would tank up beforehand.

So far so good. I could convince myself that although I drank a lot and even tanked up on occasion there was no way I was an alcoholic and so I didn't need help and I didn't need to do anything about my drinking. In fact looking at my answers to the above five questions I never considered I had an actual problem at all.

Question six loomed large in my mind however and was best avoided, it being a constant allusion to the fact that I might just have that problem, and might just possibly be an alcoholic after all.

Question six

Yes, I would **always** plan my day around drink. Even

if this was to be a day I would be unable to have a drink, as soon as I woke up I would start the process of compartmentalising my day and deciding where or where not drink could fit in. Generally my thinking for a Saturday might go thus:

'We can go shopping, then I will have a swim. We will get back about two in the afternoon and as I have been swimming I can deserve a drink. I will start with cider as the wine otherwise won't last long and no one can easily tell how much is left in a large three litre cider bottle. There is a bottle of wine for the evening in the fridge but that isn't quite enough so I will buy another bottle; but then if I have some of the new bottle that only leaves half a bottle for Sunday and I don't want to have to go to the off licence again as that looks bad and it will make me feel awkward and like an alcoholic; so I will buy two bottles today giving three for the weekend. Then it's Monday and I can go to the wine bar at lunchtime.

All this thought process might only take a second or two but it was essential for me to have planned out so I could enjoy the rest of the day.

If it was a work day I would think to myself 'who can I meet at lunchtime for a drink'. If I was meeting a client who didn't drink much or meeting someone new who might not like a drink I would generally take a fellow member of staff with me who did drink, so I would have the excuse to order a bottle of wine rather than just a glass. And when that bottle was gone, another one.

If it was the weekend and for some reason due to bad planning I had run out of drink, I might come up with the idea of drink as a reward for achieving something and as an excuse to go and buy some more. I might say to my wife 'Well, that's the shed painted and looking nice, I think that deserves a little celebration'. And if we were going out for the evening anywhere by car, I would offer to drive there knowing I could encourage my wife (who drinks little if at all) to drive back. I would also suggest we go wherever we were going as early as possible so I could have that drink earlier.

Even if I couldn't have a drink, I would know exactly when my next drink would be coming so I could look forward to it and even sometimes count down the hours, and I would always know how much drink I had in the house and ensure there was sufficient for me to rarely risk running out. I found just knowing there was an unopened bottle of wine in the fridge should I need it, a great comfort.

I don't think one day went by when I didn't let when and where I was going to have a drink dictate how I was going to organise and run my day. But it is only now I don't drink that I appreciate just how much of an issue this really was. The fact that I never ever even think about having a drink has left me with so much extra available positive thinking time, and so massively free and unrestrained in how I manage my day. I can't believe I spent so many decades of my life being beholden to alcohol. I can now do what I want, when I want, wherever I want and how I want.

> **So yes, I now recognise that I <u>was</u> an alcoholic**

I still hate the term alcoholic however and even found writing this chapter difficult because I had to admit to being one to do it. It's why I called the book 'I don't drink!' That phrase is positive, it looks to the future, and it describes my position now and going forward forever. If someone today asked me 'were you or are you an alcoholic', I would simply say 'that's irrelevant,

I don't drink!'

Why are you giving up drink, and why did I?

Important

Either as you are reading this chapter or directly afterwards you need to find a notepad and write down your own reasons as a reminder for later

Firstly you need to focus on a **big negative reason** for giving up drink, something fundamental you want to change or eliminate forever. This may be to get rid of a self-induced illness like I had; it may be to get rid of diabetes (although I didn't know my diabetes would go when I gave up drink); it may be to save your relationship; it may be to save your health and ultimately your life - only you know. Make the big negative something significant and easily identifiable that you can encompass in one word (e.g. Gout, Family, health, Life) and that you can always bring immediately to mind if you are ever tempted to have a drink and need to remind yourself why you gave it up. This one word can become the focus of a **talisman** if you decide you need one, which is discussed in the next chapter. You may of course have a whole host of big negative reasons, but I want you to focus on the biggest, the main one which may well be driving all the others in any event.

You also need **some positive reasons**, things you hope to change for the better and things you can look forward to achieving. Far more positive things will happen to you than you can possibly imagine at this stage, so update this list as things in your life start to change. I have included within the day pages of this book three email attachments I sent to my daughters at strategic points in the early days of not drinking. I sent them because I was so thrilled with the progress I was making and so proud of myself as you will deserve to be, and I wanted to share it with them. I was also so amazed at how long the list became. If you take the time to scan through these as you come across them, you will see for yourself how the list of achievements has just continued to grow. Hopefully you can feel the excitement and delight I felt in writing them.

Do you ever feel anxious or frustrated with yourself for no apparent reason? I did. That background anxiety simply melted away once I gave up drink. Perhaps it was guilt. Perhaps deep inside I knew I was putting off something I <u>had</u> to do.

What were my own pre-defined reasons?

My big negative

Of all the negative things drink was causing in my life, the biggest negative I could grasp on to was that I knew drinking was giving me gout. This in turn was making me feel old and decrepit (I couldn't run, I limped often, I was in pain which made it hard to smile, I couldn't kneel down, I couldn't walk bare foot and had to have cushioned pads in my shoes, and basically I was a physical wreck). I even began comparing myself to my deceased elder brother and thinking that as long as I lived longer than he had lived I would have achieved something. As you know I watched my brother die age 56 with a failed liver through being an alcoholic, to therefore set myself a target of living until age 57 and thinking this would be some kind of achievement was utterly pathetic. I knew when he died that enough was enough and that things had to start changing, although even then, despite the fact I cut down my drinking to an extent, it took two more years for the reality to really sink in and for me to give up completely.

I had thought about giving up drink countless times but I hadn't discussed giving up drink with anyone (they wouldn't have believed me anyway). Then at Christmas 2012 I woke up on the 30th of December with a major hangover and with acute gout in the knees. I got so angry with myself I made the immediate decision this had to really be it and I would never drink again, and I spent that entire day lost in thought, finally coming up with the bones of an idea how to achieve my new aim, and that idea became the methodology I set out in this book. Had I also known in advance how my life would be so fantastically changed for the better by giving up drink I definitely would have given it up years before, but no-one was around offering me that advice at the time, and this book hadn't been written. This is what I wrote down that day and then later put into a word document to print and pin on my wall:-

Do I want to go back to limping everywhere again?

Do I want to have stiff and swollen knees again?

Do I want to feel like I've sprained my wrist again?

Do I want my wife saying I'm like some old man again?

Do I really want the tendonitis symptoms back?

Do I want all that pain and misery back again?

JUST ONE GLASS OF WINE OR CIDER AND IT WILL ALL COME FLOODING BACK - SO NO! NEVER AGAIN! EVER!

So what is this horror called gout and how long had I been suffering from this complaint, and denying it having been caused by my drinking?

Gout is a condition caused by excess uric acid in the blood. This creates crystals in the joint which restrict movement and cause pain. My mother often had acute gout and compared the pain to childbirth.

I first had gout when I was in my early thirties and was drinking a lot of spirits. The doctor I saw diagnosed gout and gave me a course of treatment to make the symptoms go away. He put the cause down to stress as I was running my own fairly high-profile consultancy business. I did read that gout was also called the 'rich man's disease' caused by red wine and rich foods but as I wasn't rich, didn't drink red wine and only ate fairly bland food I dismissed drink as a likely cause.

Over the years I would have increasing bouts of swollen toe, swollen knees and tendonitis symptoms which were both painful and inconvenient. Many a holiday I would be found limping along beside my wife and blaming the problem on some old sports injury or early arthritis. My wife knew what it was however, she knew it was still gout and what was causing it but I refused to listen. The symptoms were especially bad if I had become dehydrated through drinking too much alcohol and no other fluids.

Sometimes I would seek help from a physiotherapist, especially for the tendonitis symptoms which would always be blamed on over-exertion at swimming, wearing the wrong shoes, having the wrong bed, sitting in the wrong position or even walking across London Bridge too fast! No specialist ever linked the tendonitis to gout or to excessive drinking. The limping was also getting worse as I was getting older and becoming an acute embarrassment.

Wherever I went I would take a packet of anti-inflammatory tablets with me, or a packet of super strength gout tablets or sometimes both. I would also have a couple of support bandages in my luggage to help alleviate swollen joints.

Finally in late 2012 I was seeing my local doctor about my type 2 diabetes and she suggested checking me for arthritis as I had swollen knees again and what felt like a sprained wrist (I even blamed the latter on excessive wallpapering would you believe!) On a whim I asked her to do a uric acid blood test as well. Sure enough I had no trace of arthritis but very high uric acid. The penny finally dropped and it was the beginning of the end for the gout!

So now I would only need to focus on that one negative reason, gout – and I made it loom huge in my subconscious so it would come and hit me like a hammer if I was ever to waver. Do I really want to go back to being an old man before my time and limping everywhere in pain, and letting this curable condition ruin my life?

Some of the big positive reasons

I had recently moved to live by the sea in a small southern English coastal town. Although I still commuted to the City most days, I desperately wanted to be as healthy in old age as many of the new friends I have made amongst the folk who spend much of their time on the seashore. I was now surrounded not by city businessmen who considered sixty-five years of age a good innings, but by men in their seventies and eighties who are all still active, mostly fit, and all certainly more mobile than I was. I am far younger than these guys and I wanted to look and feel that way. It was embarrassing when some old men asked me to help them launch their heavy fishing boat and I had to pretend to be young and fit and hide the fact I was limping and in great pain.

- I wanted to enter unknown territory and experience life at my age where drink played no part at all – what would it be like, what would happen to me, what would I do, and what would I achieve.

- I wanted to be able to do things when I wanted to do them, and not be dictated to by when I was going to have a drink and what that limited me to doing and not doing.

- I wanted to do something really positive only I could do and show myself that I had the ability to change my own life, by myself.

- Most of all, I wanted to change my life by focusing on the next thirty years as being full of health, vitality, fun and success and if I didn't achieve these things it would be through no fault of my own. Old age for me would be when I was in my nineties. I even have a next-door neighbour who lives by himself, looks after himself and still does his own gardening and he's ninety-two!

Now write down your own reasons.

One big negative reason and as many realistic positive ones as you can at this stage.

By the way;

I now have two friends I go ocean kayaking with whenever the weather permits. One of them is 27 years old and the other is 77 years old!

When should you start?

This is a big decision, especially as assuming you have not already had a drink today, this could be day one of the rest of your life and you will never touch alcohol again.

You probably have mixed feelings about when to start. On the one hand there is the excitement that you are going to do something so positive, and on the other there is the nagging doubt that you will want to keep it up as in the back of your mind you feel there will be times when a drink would be so nice to have.

Don't put the decision off. You have got this far in the book, so just do it!

You have to focus on the positive and take it from me that one day soon you will reach the stage where you will not want an alcoholic drink, ever. If you have given up smoking you will already know that after a long time has passed, the thought of having a cigarette repulses you and that thinking to yourself a cigarette would be nice is unlikely to ever happen and if it does it is just a passing fancy and a fleeting memory from the past, as untouchable as one of those

TV adverts that probably got you smoking in the first place.

The big difference between smoking and drinking is that **alcohol is not addictive** like nicotine. Your body will not think it needs alcohol. If you do get the shakes or feel strange it is more likely to be through dehydration or lack of sugar so drink lots of water and eat something sweet. Who cares at this stage if you scoff loads of chocolate bars as long as you don't have any alcohol?

Yes, you will imagine yourself in situations that will make you think about drink. For example you might be watching a movie or an advert on TV and see a situation where someone is relaxing outside a wooden cabin by a lake, looking at the distant snow-capped mountains and holding a nice crystal cut glass of whiskey. That might spark a memory as it would for me even though I haven't had a whiskey for at least thirty years. Luckily I can quickly imagine how much nicer it would be to be relaxing with a nice cup of tea, knowing the glass of whiskey would lead to too much whiskey, a muddled evening, stress that there isn't enough whiskey in the bottle to last until bedtime, and a headache in the morning assuming I wake up before lunchtime. Sticking to the tea I will wake with a fresh head, full of energy and raring to go for a walk in the wonderful morning mountain air.

I hate those beer adverts which show a nice frosted glass containing a shiny golden lager with a frothy head and people smiling and enjoying a refreshing quench after a hard day water skiing or whatever. At first they bothered me and set me off to have something refreshing as well – tea. But now I see them I realise they are just encouraging people like you and me to go back to a scenario we are escaping from. We can't just have the one refreshing beer and call it a day can we? We will stay at the bar having glass after glass and then tomorrow the drinking will start all over again. I now shout at the adverts instead, 'don't do it you fools!' which amuses my friends no end.

You have to be really strong because this is it – forever!

If you have already consumed even the tiniest drop of alcohol today, then day one might start tomorrow when you wake up, although in all likelihood you will probably want to read more of this book before you commit yourself. Either way, you should decide right **now** when you are going to give up (e.g. next Monday morning) and **set that date firmly in concrete.**

By the way, I don't believe in doing things by halves, cutting down your drinking over a period and working towards some big day that will probably never happen. What I can say for certain, is that giving something up completely is so much easier than slowly cutting down, knowing you have some self-inflicted sword of Damocles looming over you.

So now you've decided when, and you already have your key reasons well thought out you need to get a few other things in place to help you.

Turn to the next chapter and let's explore my methodology.

My methodology

Most important of all you need a system to work with – and here is my proven methodology

The methodology came about quite by accident. In writing down and thoroughly enjoying mentally reliving my drinking stories I came to realise I can laugh and chuckle at the merry times I have had being tipsy or even drunk, but without needing a drink to take me back there. I can picture the situations I was in, see myself being really silly or doing ludicrous things and even feel what it felt like at the time but almost as if I am watching myself in a film. I really can be drunk in my mind purely on memories, and without any of the negative effects.

It was this new found knowledge coupled with a desire to give up drink anyway, and knowing I had willpower (we will come on to that) that convinced me I could give up just like that 'cold turkey', and never touch another drop.

You have to believe that it is not your body that is going to want a drink, it is your mind, and so your mind is what you have to work on most and that's what we cover in the section, 'getting your mind on side'.

In addition there are a number of things I list in this chapter that helped me and that will help you give up drink, such as more exercise, an alternative interest, even mundane things such as a daily star chart which really helped cement for me what I was achieving. But the real hard work has to be in changing your attitude to drink and convincing yourself you really don't need it, because you really don't!

Check list of the things you will need to support you

I have broken the list down into essential items and things I strongly recommend. Of the latter some are easier than others to achieve. Look at the list.

You have hopefully already decided on your start date so I have ticked that box for you. You will have already listed down and focused on the one big negative reason for giving up and hopefully some positive reasons, so once again I have ticked those off for you.

For each additional item you will find a section in the next few pages, but primarily I want you to concentrate on the really essential element of my methodology which is **getting your mind on side**.

Level of importance	Item	Started?
Essential	Decide on start date	√
	Write down your big negative reason for giving up	√
	Write down some positive reasons for giving up	√
	Getting your mind on your side (Start recording your memories)	
	Willpower	
	Establish somewhere to make additional lists	
Recommended - easy	Create a star chart	
	Build a spreadsheet	
	Check your weight	
	Adopt a talisman	
Recommended - harder	Take up a new interest	
	Increase your level of physical activity	

Getting your mind on your side

There are thankfully an ever decreasing number of times when I have thought to myself, 'a drink would be nice'. It is true to say that never has this thought been brought on by the physical need for alcohol, but always by some association with a place or an event where I had in the past been either merry or drunk and consequently had a great time.

A classic example may be something as simple as my wife suggesting we go to a county agricultural show and my very first thought being 'what's the point, last time we went I could go straight to the cider stall, get a little tipsy, and then walk around the show in a nice relaxed fashion with a drink in my hand. This time it would just be bloody tea or water.'

What has helped me at such times, and to get me over that negative thought (which does only last a second or two) is to force myself to remember that last time when I was there and **did** have a glass in my hand. I mentally picture myself walking round tiddly and with a stupid grin on my face, and then tell myself I don't actually have to have the actual drink with me to feel as I did. I can be just as merry, but with all the additional advantages of a much happier wife with far fewer reasons to be cross with me, have both hands free as I walk around the show and not worry about spilling anything, not have to think about where the next top-up is coming from, have nothing to stop me from driving home because I will be completely sober, and know I will have zero after affects. In fact I know I will be enjoying myself just as much as last time but being far happier about it, because I have already **been there and done that!**

If suggesting you think about drinking seems somewhat bizarre and contradictory to what most 'giving up alcohol' programmes suggest, what I am actually doing is creating in my memory banks a happily drunken state for myself without having to have a drink. I am giving myself the comfort factor that I have '**been there and done that**' already, and so don't need to go there again, thank-you.

This might sound complex, but it doesn't take much practice to do this and the result is that within a few seconds it is as if you have gone from wanting a drink (very different from needing a drink, which you physically don't), to being as if you have had a drink and feel nicely relaxed and calm. It is like having a conversation with yourself where you ask yourself 'Surely you will miss having a nice cold beer watching the world go by?' and answering, 'No, I've already done that, I don't physically need a beer so I'm quite happy not having one and having something non-alcoholic instead'. After all, having already been there and done that, you are not missing out this time, are you? Instead you are one step further away from the old you with all the negative drink related issues, and one giant step nearer to the new you free from all that terrible baggage.

So rather than hide from drink and avoiding thinking about drink I am from memory creating the ability to place myself in a situation where I have enjoyed that drink and so immediately not want one in reality, it's a bit like time travel without having to physically go anywhere.

It is a complete 'been there done that' scenario bottled in my memory banks and that I can bring out and use whenever I feel the need.

Been there – done that!

I realise now that writing my first book was a way of expunging within me the desire for a drink by writing down amusing stories from the time before I was old enough to drink, to events involving lots of drink, and to other events where I had an incredible amount of fun and drink didn't feature once. As you read some of my stories and experiences in this book hopefully they will remind you of similar experiences of your own. Hopefully you too will be able to chuckle and think 'I remember being that drunk, what a nightmare' and be able to say to yourself, 'yes, I have been there and done that too, so I don't need to go there again either.'

When people who have known me a long time ask me why I have given up drinking sometimes I will even say, 'because I have been there, I have done that, and I am now doing something else instead.' It really is like casting off an old skin, and not hating it for having been there, but remembering the good and bad things about wearing it, but never wanting to put it back on again.

So how do you go about it?

I am aware in some therapy sessions they make you list all the bad things about drink and focus on these, and initially it will help you to have your one key reason for giving up drink to focus on. As discussed, for me it was having gout. I knew I had gout despite my blaming the symptoms on sports injuries and other causes, and I secretly knew it was caused by excessive drinking and could therefore be stopped.

But more importantly I want to encourage you to remember some fun times that involved lots of drink. Preferably these will be times where you know you drank to excess and although you had a great time you suffered for it later, either physically through a hangover and feeling like death or some other sort of comeuppance. I want you to be able to think of events and times where you can remember how it felt to be merrily drunk so you don't actually need a physical drink to make you feel the same way. You might want to pick a selection of experiences, such as being tipsy and a bit silly, to being pissed and having a maniac time with mates, and to being far too drunk and knowing the day fell apart for you. Try and avoid anything really awful such as being in the depths of despair because you won't be going there again will you.

I want you to list these down and make some notes about what happened and how you felt, both at the time and afterwards. I want you to be able to bullet these notes into thoughts that make you smile and that will remind you what it is like to be a little drunk in various situations because then you don't need to have an actual drink this time. You can imagine one glass of wine making you feel relax and so feel relaxed, you can imagine five glasses of wine making you feel a bit too sloshed and so remember what it feels like to be sloshed but switch away and be immediately sober.

I found writing the stories down the best way of getting these scenarios fixed in my subconscious. Have a read of one and you might see how they work – try the 'Ballroom Blitz'. This started off as a series of simple notes about my most embarrassing moment ever as a result of alcohol.

If you don't think you can write, how about drawing a picture that reminds you of that event, or paint a picture, or create a cartoon or even record something. At the very least you could make some notes. But whatever you do (unless you are like me and are happy to publish things for the world to read) keep them tucked away somewhere secret but where you can access them and read/look/listen to them if you think you really do want a drink. Hopefully if you are anything like me, just thinking about that time will bring a smile to your face and take away any mental craving because after all that is only what it is. It is purely your mind saying I enjoyed being drunk and I want to be drunk again – you really don't need the physical alcohol to appease your subconscious.

All you need to do is spur a memory; after a few times your brain will take over and in a flash as if drowning, all those scenarios will race through your mind and you won't want a drink this time! All those experiences, smells, tastes, and feelings are there in your memory-banks, they will never go. So you have already been there and done that and can therefore do so again whenever you want – you just have to let your mind do some focusing for you.

So have a think now what you could write or record. Make a few notes that you can expand on either before you start not drinking, or in the first few days so as not to put off that all important start date. It might seem that I am asking a lot of you, after all you just want to give up alcohol and are probably looking for some magic to help, but having some of your drinking memories to look back on and remind yourself that you have 'been there and done that' really will help more than anything that could be conjured up. If you really struggle to put anything down by all means use my stories as a fall back, but your own stories based on your own experiences will be a million times better.

Just to remind you, there are more of my stories for you to read on-line or download for free at my website:

www.idontdrink.net

And one further thought here, you are lucky because you **do** have those memories to help you. If you were reading this book never having been a drinker or having been drunk, you might be wondering what all the fuss is about!

The next most essential thing - Willpower

WILLPOWER

A lot of people say to me I must have amazing willpower to just give up drinking, and how much they would like to do the same if only they had my willpower. So what is willpower and have you got any?

There are endless books available on the subject of willpower, and guides that promise to help you develop your willpower by using meditation and focusing on the 'self', but most of these involve many months of practice and so are of little use to those of us like you that want to give up drinking now!

Put basically, willpower is simply having the **determination** to achieve something, but sometimes you need a little help and some self-belief! Some of that 'I can do it' attitude.

If you look back at your life there will be numerous occasions when you had to exercise willpower. It might be when you gathered together the courage to start a conversation with someone you fancied and who became your first boy or girlfriend - that took willpower. I remember how long it took me to summon together the courage to make that first phone call and ask a girl for a date, the stress was enormous but I did it. Managing to cope with a job interview or even struggling through your driving test took willpower. So we all have willpower, it sometimes just needs to be brought to the surface and focused. Even opening and commencing to read this book took a lot of willpower, for a start you have had to recognise and accept that you have a problem. You have also obviously made the decision you want to do something about it, and that also took willpower. So tell yourself now that you are determined to give up drinking forever.

My own focused willpower became more consciously developed as a result of being in the Territorial Army.

The military are expert at making you achieve the seemingly impossible, whether this be facing an armed and hostile foe during war time, or convincing yourself you will be able to get over a twelve foot wall as part of an assault course in peacetime. The NCO's with their threats and banter somehow manage to instil in you a belief that you can conquer any obstacle that comes your way, and leave you with a blind faith in your own ability. The Army does not accept 'can't' as an answer.

My introduction to the territorials was on an induction weekend with my elder brother Paul who had decided to join up with me. At our local TA centre we were made to don a non-descript khaki uniform, thrown into the back of a four tonner truck along with many other potential recruits and driven to a Hampshire barracks to test our suitability as one-day cannon fodder. After much hanging around in cold barren rooms waiting for something to happen (much of Army life is apparently like this) the physical element of our induction involved running three miles in less than twenty-five minutes, a martial arts session where you were made to fight each other, and having to complete an enormous assault course in two teams, with each team carrying a telegraph pole throughout. To say that not one of us believed we could ever achieve these tasks and live to tell the tale is an understatement. But we did achieve them, and my brother managed to see it through despite having broken a rib early on in the gym! What helped us through this ordeal was a heavy dose of army gung-ho mentality, lots of shouting and abuse from violent looking sergeants who convinced us that even young schoolgirls could do better than we were doing (and I'm sure they probably could), the khaki uniform that somehow mentally allied us to every war-film hero we had ever seen and who we desperately wanted to emulate, and the team spirit the NCO's engendered which meant that none of us wanted to let the others down. We were made to 'Think Army'.

A similar story could be told by my eldest daughter who joined the officer Training Corps when at University. Despite her trepidation on having to do a parachute jump on one of her training weekends, when it came to the day and she was standing by the open door at three thousand feet looking down, she had no hesitation in leaping from the aircraft when ordered to do so by the sergeant in charge – she was made to 'Think Army', and engendering that Army mentality really does give you an inner belief that you can accomplish anything you set your mind to.

Ever since those Territorial Army days I have carried that slogan with me, I even have a t-shirt with the words emblazoned across it:-

THINK ARMY

Whenever I have to face a difficult or stressful situation I think of that phrase and take to the task as if a fearsome army sergeant has been watching my every move and telling me I can and will do this thing. I actually say to myself 'Think Army' and bristle with determination to go and get the job done whatever the consequences. Such occasions have included diverse situations such as public speaking both on a business and personal level and sometimes to very large audiences; launching a kayak into a rough and turbulent sea with a crowd watching from the beach and expecting me to drown and me not wanting to back down; crossing a rickety rope bridge suspended high in the canopy of the Malaysian jungle despite a massive fear of heights because I didn't want to lose out on the experience; and of course giving me that 'I can do this' confidence when giving up both smoking and drinking because I knew it was the right thing to do and I didn't want to fail. The Army doesn't let you fail.

You probably haven't been as lucky as I have and had some military experience, but that doesn't matter. Think of someone you admire for their strength of character and their sense of purpose, someone you would wish to emulate, possibly a sports person or a famous explorer. It doesn't have to be a living person or someone from history, it doesn't even have to be a real person. It could just as easily be a movie hero or a hero in a novel, but think of someone who wouldn't give up, someone who would see things through to the end and achieve their goal. Try and think of someone you can bring to mind if you start to falter in your resolve, and be able to think to yourself 'he or she wouldn't back down and have a drink. They would be strong so I will be just as strong!' Or you can borrow my own slogan and 'Think Army'.

Another good way to strengthen your resolve is to look at your star chart (see next chapter) and think about how much you have achieved so far. Do you really want to throw all that success away and go back to being a drunk, or to have to start the process all over again? Do you really want to tear up your chart and delete your spreadsheet because you have failed? In my mind there is little point in just skipping a day and then carrying on as normal, because that just allows you to skip yet another day later on, and so on. I know that because that is exactly what happened to me many years ago when I gave up smoking and cut down drinking at the same time.

Also, think of that hero I mentioned two paragraphs ago, wouldn't you be disappointed if you met your hero in real life and they turned out to be a fraud. So don't cheat yourself, you do have the willpower and consequently the determination to see this through. And remember, once you give up alcohol, it really won't be long before you will start to hate the thought of having a drink, so stick with it!

Team spirit

Finally, I mentioned the Army instil in you a team spirit that helps you find hidden strengths and resolve. Once you let people get to know you have given up drinking you are likely to develop a fan base, friends and family who will actively tell others who much they admire what you have achieved and use you as an example of someone to look up to. By that stage you will also have brought your partner or best friend on side as well. Add these people to your virtual team working to help you achieve your goal, you certainly wouldn't want to let them down, would you?

Some additional lists to make

As discussed in the chapter 'why are you giving up drink', before or even on your **start day**, I asked you to list the big negative reason and all the positive reasons you are giving up drink and keep the list up to date. You might want to make a poster with regard to the big negative reason like I did.

Now there are three further lists I would ask you to make and to keep active:-

- List all the positive things that happen to you once you give up drink and keep this list up to date. I include within the day pages of this book three of my lists, all put together at different stages as e-mails to send to my daughters both because I was so proud of myself and so amazed by all the wonderful changes taking place, and as a gentle pointer to them and their husbands not to become as reliant on drink as I had. As you come across these you will see for yourself how the number of items just keeps on growing.

- As more and more non-drinking days pass, you will quickly realise just how much of a damned nuisance drinking was. List as many things as you can about drinking that really annoyed you or gave you stress. Have a read of my list in the chapter **'drink related scenarios and a new found freedom'** and see how many you have an affinity with and that touch a nerve with you.

- Log your thoughts. I made notes as things sprang into my head. Even if this was 'saw someone drinking an ice cold glass of Sancerre and was really tempted', just writing that down and then supplementing it with, 'I would have turned that one glass into two bottles, a huge amount of self-belief down the drain and hated myself the next day when I woke up with the first tingling sensation of gout returning, tore up my star chart and went back to being a drunk, but even more miserable than before'.

Other things you are going to need

Highly recommended

Here are a few other things that can really help you. Some of these are straightforward, some less so and all are optional although I would recommend you adopt all if possible.

> **None of these should take more than a few minutes to think about and can be organised quite simply – so do NOT let them be an excuse for delaying your start date**

Create a star chart

I got hold of a wall calendar, marked in large pen the day I was going to start and then made a point of adding a star to the chart every day. Although you could say this is childish and a bit basic, it is fun and you will be amazed how much pleasure you get every morning sticking on a star knowing that is yet another day of no drink successfully accomplished. The best part was turning over the page having completed a whole month and knowing I was entering territory very few of my friends had been, even the ones who say they give up drinking for one whole month every year. Once you get used to adding a star every day you will hate the thought of having to miss one out because you had even the tiniest sip of alcohol. In my book, once you don't drink, any alcohol at all means total failure and back to the start you go, I even avoid Christmas cake and other foods that might have added alcohol.

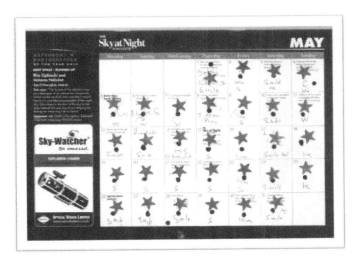

As you will see from the photograph of my chart, there are a few other things I mark each day as well. These include a red dot my wife started adding when she gave up smoking (my giving up drinking encouraged her to similarly challenge herself and she has managed a whole year now); a K every time I go out on my kayak; a Ka for a karate lesson; an S when I have been swimming (becomes Smile if I swim a mile that day); and other activities I want to celebrate having completed such as the local charity ocean raft race or an organised walk over 6 miles in length.

To be honest, I am now past the stage where I need to mark my progress as I am completely confident I don't need this self-rewarding technique, but it does give me a positive lift every morning so I expect I will continue forever.

By the way, the 'Sky at Night' calendar does give away the fact I love stargazing. It is so much easier now I can set my alarm for the early hours and wake up feeling fresh and keen to see what is up there in the cosmos on show. I also don't fall over in the dark anymore or spill wine all over my clothes and the telescope housing!

Build a spreadsheet

The star chart quickly became something more sophisticated and I created a very simple spreadsheet version to maintain as well. The picture below shows a section from mine.

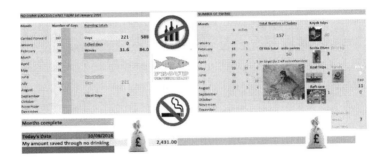

The advantages of this approach are many and include:-

- The chart automatically maintains a running total of days, weeks and months achieved to date.
- I have taken an average of how much I used to spend on alcohol per day and the chart maintains a running total of how much I have saved (this amounts up at an alarming rate).

- I have added running totals of distance swum, number of activities undertaken etc. just because it's nice to know.

You may want to keep a paper log of how well you are doing instead, but in any event do maintain something. It is very very satisfying especially in the early days to be able to say to yourself or your partner, 'I have done 50 days without a drink already and saved £550. I've also swum 35 miles!'

I also made a point of adding a 'failed days' total which I was determined to keep at zero. It would have been horrible to have had to log even one day in this section, thus undermining all the other work to date. I would have been prepared to press the delete button and kill the spreadsheet if I failed. But just having it there was a further incentive never to fail.

I have provided a template spreadsheet and a full example of my own on my website for you to download and use should you wish.

www.idontdrink.net

Check your weight

I have lost 28 pounds (12.7 kilos) purely giving up drink and taking more exercise. This is despite the fact I am eating more as I feel hungrier and I have also developed a sweet tooth, eating biscuits and cakes to make up for the sugar I am not getting in the drink. In fact I never used to eat puddings but now have a treacle sponge pudding and ice cream every night and it makes no difference to my weight! Losing unnecessary weight feels great, especially as you start to trim down so it would be a shame not to log your weight at the start. I have now plateaued at a steady 80 kilos with a BMI of 24 which is well into the healthy area for someone of my height. Regardless of what I do activity wise or what I eat this never seems to change so I am happy to remain at this level. Incidentally, it took about three months to lose all this weight and that was without trying!

If like me you also suffer (did suffer) from high blood pressure, you may want to check your level before you start as well. If you are on medication this may be at normal level, but I found my blood pressure reduce dramatically after giving up alcohol and it only returned to normal once I stopped taking the tablets. You should of course only do this after taking advice from your doctor as I did.

Adopt a talisman

Imagine a situation where you are sitting or standing in a crowd and someone is either handing round drinks or asking everyone in turn what they want to drink. It might be stressful waiting your opportunity to say 'I don't drink', and you might even be tempted to take a glass or order a small drink instead just to be polite (I know people who have done just that). Similarly, imagine being in a high stress situation such as in the middle of a blazing row with your partner or children/parents/boss, the sort of situation which might in the past have driven you to think 'sod it' and go off and have a drink. What you really need at a time like this is someone sitting on your shoulder whispering in your ear, 'Remember, you don't drink! Remember why you don't drink!'

Unfortunately no-one has to date invented a small shoulder sized person plugged into your brain, so instead why not create your own little talisman to have with you in a pocket or handbag and that you can squeeze by way of a reminder and point of focus when needed.

This rather worn looking pebble is what I carried with me for the first few weeks and then kept by my bedside as a reminder once any chance of my relapsing had completely gone away. You can see I have written the word GOUT on it, (as well as some other words added when I was bored) the idea being that if I was tempted to have a drink, I would squeeze the stone kept in my pocket and remind myself of the one big negative reason for giving up drink, focusing all my negative energy into the stone and so relieving myself of any 'desire for a drink' related stress. Far better to pour your negative waves into the talisman than into a glass of misery.

In actual fact although I carried the stone with me I never needed to use it as any thought of having an alcoholic drink evaporated away so soon after starting giving up it became unnecessary. You might not be so lucky however so don't chance it and think about making something of your own, anything will do.

In case you are wondering what gave me this strange idea in the first place, it all came about as part of my Open University geoscience course and the first exam I had to sit. Passing this exam was key to the course and it was the first I had sat since leaving school some thirty-five years before, so I was understandably nervous and suffering from exam stress. Fortunately the week before I had attended a weekend exam workshop where a wonderful tutor took us through the format of the test we were to sit. She explained that as it was a geology paper, 10% of the marks would be awarded for correctly identifying a mystery rock we would be given in a velvet bag to be opened when the allotted time commenced. She advised that before we even looked at the exam paper we should open the bag, glance at the rock, hold it in our hand, and squeeze it as we calmly read through the rest of the questions. She surmised that by the time we had finished reading not only would we have focused more on understanding the questions and therefore starting the grey matter working on solutions, but that our brain would also have identified the rock and we could start the paper with 10% of the marks to our credit, which given the minimum pass mark was only 40% we would be well on the way to success. Her strategy worked for all of us who attended that weekend workshop and I managed a 90% pass.

Incidentally when I finally publish this book I will have managed in excess of two years without a single drop of alcohol, and I intend to throw that stone back into the ocean, just by way of turning my back on any negative aspects of my past, and focusing even more on the wonderful time I am having, and the future that lies waiting for me. Far better to chuck the stone away than lose it and get all superstitious about it!

A new or revised interest

You are going to have far more free time on your hands, and depending upon your physical state at the start you will become far more active and have a hugely increased stamina. You need to keep yourself busy.

An evening based hobby is ideal if you can spare the time, preferably something you have to drive to or be completely sober to undertake. I increased my swimming at first but once I had lost weight and increased my level of fitness I took up karate as well, something I had always wanted to do but never had the time or the energy. I also walk one or two times per day and for between half an hour and an hour each time. This provides fantastic thinking time as well as keeping me fit and led to me completing my first book!

In the past when I wanted to cut down my drinking I took up evening classes driving to the next village for pottery class one evening per week. Although this helped for that one evening however, it didn't help at other times so you do need something that is going to be available to you every day. That is why a physical activity is best, although you might find even reading or doing a home study course will be sufficient. Even though it didn't lead to me giving up drinking (I hadn't decided I needed to at that stage) I found undertaking an Open University science course stimulating and fulfilling and it took up every spare hour I could find. It even led to me getting my BSc Honours degree in Geosciences just five years ago!

> I went a bit crossword and Sudoku mad in the first few weeks just to have something to keep my mind active. It's a bit like when people give up smoking and they need to keep their hands busy.

Or you could write a book like I did, after all they say everyone has a book inside them and with self-publishing being so straightforward these days, why not have a go? Mine is a whole collection of amusing short stories based on events in my life. You can find some stories from it on my book website at **www.the752tolondonbridge.com**

Physical activity

I think having some form of physical activity to help you is absolutely essential but I've placed it under recommended just in case of the unlikely event that your situation doesn't make taking up any form of activity possible. You need something that if you get restless and really feel you have to have a drink you can just do to take your mind completely off drink. Something to hopefully wear yourself out so you no longer want a drink, and to remind you that giving up drink is to create a new you and being far fitter and consequently happier in yourself is part of that. This is most likely to occur in the late afternoon or evening.

I took this approach when I gave up smoking 'cold turkey' fashion some twenty years ago. I started swimming each evening. Although at first I found the swimming hard work just to complete a few lengths of the pool, I would wait until the craving for a cigarette was such that I was desperate and then I would rush off to the pool, exhaust myself, and then come home to bed knowing a cigarette was the last thing I would want after a hard swimming session. I also signed up for the annual charity 'swimathon' as an added incentive. This annual 5 kilometre swim is something I now do every year as a challenge to myself, completing the swim non-stop in less than two hours which is pretty good given I only swim breaststroke. 5 kilometres is 200 lengths of the average 25 metre pool.

Ever since those days and until I gave up drink I had swum probably twice a week although I liked to think it was more. In fact the drinking got in the way as all evening swimming stopped (I would be drinking instead and couldn't drive to a pool) and I would only swim during the day at weekends, the latest time being about five o'clock after which I would want a glass to be in my hand. When I gave up drink I went back to the old regime and swam every evening for the first two months and have swum nearly every day since. What is wonderful is that I can swim whenever I feel like it as drink no longer dictates when I swim or whether I am able to drive to the pool or not. If I am not swimming it is because I am out on my kayak, I have been to the City and have arrived home after the pool has closed, or it is karate night.

If I hadn't had swimming to rely on (and a convenient local pool), I would have taken up jogging or cycling. If you are not able to undertake any strenuous exercise there are gentler, even chair based routines you can do. But you **must** do something.

You will lose weight through not drinking and you will very quickly start to feel fitter and in better health, and as your body starts to thank you for no longer poisoning it you want to return the favour and make yourself even fitter still. Even if you have a busy schedule, if you were drinking every day the drinking you were doing took time, so you can now replace that time doing something positive, and with a completely clear head.

You do have the time

So use it to better yourself

Summary

Now put together the things you are going to need. Make a decision on the activity you are going to pursue and make any arrangements if necessary. This might include buying some new sports gear or finding the gear you used to wear, or it might just involve deciding now at which time every evening you are going to go for a long walk and to where. Whatever your new schedule is going to be, decide now. You can always change it of course as long as you continue to do something every day. And please don't use the expense of joining a Gym as an excuse to do nothing, walking is free.

The check list again

I here repeat the check list for you to complete. Do note however that most of the items are for completion and expansion as you progress through the early days of not drinking. Please don't let not having any of these items ready beforehand stop you deciding on a date, or even starting to stop drinking as of today, after all, as for recording your memories you can always start by adopting my stories.

You will also note that I have additionally ticked the willpower box for you. To convince you why, I repeat the statement from the willpower section of this chapter:-

'Even opening and commencing to read this book took a lot of willpower, for a start you have had to recognise and accept that you have a problem. You have also obviously made the decision you want to do something about it, and that also took willpower. So tell yourself now that you are determined to give up drinking forever'.

Level of importance	Item	Started?
Essential	Decide on start date	√
	Write down your big negative reason for giving up	√
	Write down some positive reasons for giving up	√
	Getting your mind on your side (Start recording your memories)	
	Willpower	√
	Establish somewhere to make additional lists	
Recommended - easy	Create a star chart	
	Build a spreadsheet	
	Check your weight	
	Adopt a talisman	
Recommended - harder	Take up a new interest	
	Increase your level of physical activity	

Now you are almost ready to press start, but first let's cover three things that tend to crop up:-

- **What do you tell other people, and when?**

- **What can you expect to feel?**

- **What else did I (might you) have to give up?**

What do you tell other people, and when?

First of all I wouldn't tell anyone you have given up drink for at least a week, perhaps not even your partner or best friend. The chances are you will have tried giving up before or cutting down and so are unlikely to be believed this time and the last thing you need right now is negative waves. Much better to say you are feeling out of sorts or to make up some other such lie to divert questions away from you at this stage.

Once you have achieved a whole week without a drink and are on the way to week two you might want to show your chart to those close to you, let them have a look at this book you are using and they can start to share in your success.

As for your friends and associates who do drink, I would leave it much longer and save revealing anything until month two. In the meantime you might want to say you are giving up for a while to lose some weight or give your system a rest from alcohol. Telling them any earlier that you have given up drink for good may get a mixed reaction:-

- *Some people will be jealous and react by saying you are mad; what is the point; you only live once so enjoy it to the full; it won't last and other such negative nonsense to try and encourage you to stay a drinker like themselves.*

- *Some people will be more receptive but want to excuse their own drinking by saying things such as 'a glass of wine per day is medically proven to be good for you'.*

- *More likely, people will say how they also gave up for a month and found it really easy, that they do it every year and how they don't have a drink problem themselves.*

To all these I have to say: how much better to live the one life we have healthy, sober, wealthier and having much more fun; there is no such thing as one glass per day, it always leads to more than that, and if it was so easy to give up why go back to drinking?

Once you have passed the magic month target, in my experience people will either not want to broach the subject with you at all, or they will show more respect and will want to know how you have managed it, will reveal the fact that they have tried but failed at some stage or certainly know someone who has. Although you may not want people looking up to you in this way (it shows how proud of you people can be for achieving such a great thing), it does make you feel virtuous and helps to ensure there is no way you can go back from this point on.

There is of course one huge advantage to proudly telling people you no longer drink once you have passed the one month stage. All those people will undoubtedly admire you and start telling other people, they know someone who used to drink and who has kicked the habit. The more the word spreads the harder it would be for you to ever go back to being a drinker. Not only would you have failed yourself but you would have let down all those believers as well. There are loads of people who know I don't drink, and I know any one of them would be so disappointed if they saw me drinking, and they would feel really let down personally. So go on, tell the World. Put the pressure on yourself because it will always be at the back of your mind if ever you should waver, and that might just be what you need to make sure you continue to say NO! In fact make them part of your virtual team.

What do you say when someone offers you a beer?

You could say 'No thanks, I'm teetotal'. This is probably a good word and an apt description of someone who doesn't partake of alcohol but to me it sounds too biblical, and in fact it harks back to nineteenth century temperance society days. It really makes me feel as if I belong to some crusading church based group who will try and convert every drinking sinner I meet. It also stinks of someone who was evilly bad and has been converted (I was a sinner who drank, then I saw the light and became a teetotal) or of someone who had to be locked away and cleaned up drug addict style. This may well be the case with you, but I still hate the terminology and prefer to simply call myself someone who doesn't drink. If I was at a party I wouldn't mind being pointed out as 'there's Julian, he doesn't drink you know', it sounds quite nice and friendly and even interesting, rather than 'there's Julian, he's a teetotal'. I think it makes me sound like someone to be avoided at all costs.

So much better to smile and say 'No thanks, I don't drink'. This will probably spark the response 'What, not at all?' To which you can proudly say yes, and when they then ask you how long this has been the case you can again proudly say x weeks, or x months or even like me, since 2012.

And the reason?

As you will have discovered in this book, I don't really harp on about all the reasons why I gave up drink, it's too depressing. I much prefer to say it doesn't matter why I gave up, let me tell you about all the fantastic things that have happened since I did give up (I feel ten years younger, I have never been so fit, I have so much more spare time to enjoy, I have taken up a new hobby, I have lost two stone, I no longer have diabetes) it is all so positive and it really helps to cement in your own mind all the wonderful reasons for having changed your life. You can only get a positive response to this approach, and that helps even more. You may even encourage someone else to quit the drink as well, I have!

It is also interesting how many people have 'just given up drinking', have cut down dramatically or rarely touch a drop anyway. This is what you will constantly hear when people notice you don't drink. Don't believe a word of it, they are all making it up because they are envious and they should be, you have achieved something fantastic. You might for instance be at a business cocktail event as I was recently, and standing there with your wine glass full of water, and people you know will come over and the conversation might go like this:

'Hi Julian, you're not drinking?'

'I don't drink anymore'

'What, just on weekends?'

'No, I have given up completely, I wanted to do something really positive, I decided enough was enough, that I'd never touch a drop again and the change since has been incredible.'

'Oh, I hardly ever drink, just at events like this

perhaps and at Christmas and Birthdays. You drink then of course?'

'No, I have given up completely, I wanted to do something really positive, I decided enough was enough, that I'd never touch a drop again and the change since has been incredible.'

'I don't think I could completely give up like that. I expect you have just the odd glass?'

'No, I have given up completely, I wanted to do something......

It seems almost everyone would like to be a non-drinker and is keen to associate themselves with your non-drinking stance albeit they might find it hard to come to terms with. There are very few who seem to completely manage it however, for whatever reasons of their own. What really scares them is when you have managed to be a non-drinker for over a year.

'I wouldn't call myself a drinker. I do the dry January thing each year, well mostly. How long have you managed now Julian?'

'Two years.'

'Sh...'

Or I tell them this one:

In 2011 I had high blood pressure, high cholesterol and was told by my doctor I had type 2 diabetes, but that if I lost weight and changed my lifestyle it might not develop. I went for my six monthly check-ups and nothing much happened. Then I gave up drink.

It's all gone!

What can you expect to feel?

There are four emotions that stand out and capture how I felt for the first few weeks of giving up drinking and before the sheer delight in my new found life took over.

Lost

The habit of what seems like a lifetime will be changed overnight. It's not like you are just having a few days off the drink or even doing a dry month for a bet or for charity, this is it forever.

Your old friend alcohol will no longer be there to act as a crutch when you think you need it. Instead you **will** find an inner strength emerge that you didn't realise or had forgotten that you had.

You will wonder where all the spare time has come from. Instead of sitting down with a drink, or going to the pub you will have more energy to do and achieve things, and far more time to do them in. But until you start to fill the time usefully you really will feel strange and lost.

You will find yourself thinking 'by now I would be doing this or doing that', all of which involved drink. Even writing this at four in the afternoon I can think 'the old me would have had a glass of wine next to me by now and probably already had most of the bottle'. Instead it still amazes me that I don't miss drink one little bit, especially as I know I would have had to completely rewrite all this again tomorrow when I was sober!

Confused

Why don't you want a drink? And if you really think about it whilst on the surface you may think you want one, deep down you really don't! That can be confusing after all these years.

Similarly, why is it so much easier to give up drink than you thought it would be? Are you missing a trick somewhere and your life is going to come crashing down? The answer is no, once you are firm in your decision it really is easy to give up – surprisingly so.

Bored

With so much free time on your hands (and you won't be spending time thinking about drink either) it can be easy to become bored. It's one of the reasons I really got into my writing, I just had so much extra time to fill, especially in the evenings. I also used to watch a film on TV most evenings and sit down with some wine to relax and probably fall asleep. I now find watching TV boring, I've got far too much energy to just sit around in front of a box. I probably watch at most one hour a week – really!

My family do complain I have become hyperactive and that I'm always on the go. That is no bad thing of course it just takes them some adjusting to. They are used to a man who would slow down in the afternoon and be happy doing nothing as long as there was a drink to be had. Now there is no stopping me!

Mentally laid back

There is a huge amount of stress which has simply melted away.

Did I mention?

Ever since I was a little boy I have had psoriasis quite badly, especially on my knees, elbows and hands. Although lots of sunshine seems to help, the condition is blamed on stress. Since giving up drink, the psoriasis has completely gone!

The very fact I no longer have to feel guilty or worry about drinking too much or too often, or where the next drink is going to come from and all that associated nightmare has eliminated a massive amount of stress. The fact I feel so well and that I am so healthy has also reduced stress to a major extent.

In fact there is nothing I can think of that I have to be stressed about, but then I am very lucky. I could try and make myself stressed about finances or my job or just plain life but I know it wouldn't work. The fact that I am not turning to drink as an excuse to relieve stress but instead dealing with any issues immediately they arise and tackling them logically makes them seem so minor compared to how I used to view things. Perhaps it's because I can cope with so much more, or perhaps there is no longer an excuse to hide and a place to hide called being drunk. And I do have pressures and situations that would have caused me untold stress before. Now I really am far more laid back about how I face things and far more philosophical.

If you think drink helps you deal with stress - think again!

It might be what people tell you and what you read but don't believe it for a second, it simply is _not_ true

What else did I (might you) have to give up?

If I have made things sound fairly straightforward, there is something quite major that I had to give up in addition to drink – **sausages!**

When I was a teenager my parents spent a great deal of time travelling and I was left 'home alone'. Fearful that I wouldn't eat properly my mother's solution was to prepare, cook and freeze countless identical dinners for me in advance. The recipe was sausages, mashed potato and beans. Consequently I became so used to this simple diet it became all that I would eat and I lost any sense of adventure with food.

This 'need' for sausages stayed with me all my adult life and grew steadily into what became an almost nightly ritual of barbecuing my sausages which was no fun for my wife. She had decided to become pescatarian (a vegetarian who also eats fish) after contracting severe dysentery following eating a chicken sandwich from a broken down fridge. In fact she became so anti-meat I wouldn't have been allowed to use the same oven or kitchen surfaces for my sausages in any event. Even in mid-winter I could be found outside happily barbecuing my sausages, I even built various shelters wherever we lived to keep off rain and snow. Now as almost anyone who drinks knows, a barbecue is a great excuse to drink, and standing in the fresh air watching my sausages brown whilst enjoying a nice bottle of white wine or downing glass after glass of cider was a real pleasure. So much so that I had to develop a taste for burnt sausages.

- Giving up drink the barbecuing had to go.
- Giving up barbecuing the sausages had to go.
- Giving up sausages, meat in general had to go.

So I also became pescatarian and have been ever since the day I gave up drink.

Now I am not suggesting for a second that you follow suit and give up meat, I only add this section for a point of interest and because changing my diet at the same time as giving up drink certainly helped me by breaking with routine. It was a bit like me giving up coffee for a few months when I gave up smoking because the two went together so well. You might just find that looking forward to that nice Sunday roast with all the trimmings that you used to wash down with a sumptuous bottle of red, just has to be put on hold for a while, or at least until you can confidently replace the red wine with something like a nice bottle of mineral water.

Incidentally for those of you who assume I now have a daily diet of lettuce and tomato with a piece of rye bread (the sort of rubbish I assumed all vegetarians lived on), here is a typical delicious weekly evening menu my wife puts together:-

	MENU
Weekly meal plan	
Monday	Vegetable melody with breaded fish
Tuesday	Pumpkin goulash with lentils and home-made crusty bread
Wednesday	Root vegetable stew and dumplings
Thursday	Butternut squash and blue cheese filo pie with jacket potatoes
Friday	Breaded fish with home-made potato wedges
Saturday	Salmon bake with jacket potatoes, beans and courgettes
Sunday	Sweet potato chilli with garlic bread

Please note: Lettuce is optional

And don't forget, I follow that up each night with a treacle pudding and ice cream, or a crumble of some description dependent upon what fruit is available, or strawberries in the summer!

What about giving up snoring?

I was always led to believe it was the drinking that made me snore so loudly, and I used to snore at such a high volume people threatened to have me put down. Now apparently they only want to have me committed!

Don't turn to the next chapter yet!

The next chapter **is** the **big start** button. Straight after that it's the night before your big first day. Unless you are simply scanning through the book at this stage, once you really and meaningfully get to the start button there is no turning back. Scaring isn't it?

This is where you need to sit quiet, think about life and stare hard at your future. This is where you internally commit to giving up drink forever. This is where you forever turn your back on that nice bottle of wine with dinner, that beer or gin with your friends, that cocktail on a summer's evening, or that late night whiskey as you page through your favourite novel.

I deliberately mention all these tempting things because you **will** be tempted once you pass start. But you have already decided you want to do this thing, so summon the strength and **go for it**. You **can** do this thing, I did. And you will **never** regret it, not for a second!

But only you can choose.

To use an analogy from the natural World, do you want to be a strong fearless sharp-eyed Eagle and spend the rest of your wonderful life in charge of your own destiny, or do you want to be a Snail carrying a world of woes on your back and heading for the nearest beer-trap to slowly kill yourself in a drink-sodden fizz?

Eagle or Snail – the choice is yours

Snails can throw the book away at this point, or give it to someone more deserving.

Fellow Eagles come fly with me to the next chapter and let's hit that big start button together

Well done!

The night before

This is the eve of the big day. Hopefully you already feel excited because just knowing you are doing something so positive and life changing should naturally make you feel special. You may also feel a little apprehensive, I have to say I didn't because I knew in my mind I was finally doing something about getting rid of gout forever and so I couldn't wait to start ticking off the days on my chart. That's why it is important to have one big negative thing to initially focus on, something specific that has to change.

Don't put tomorrow off. This really is the start, tomorrow you are going to be one of those people nearly everyone secretly admires and dreams of being, a completely happy non-drinker, and especially happy because **you** chose that path. It really will be one of the most important changes you can ever make in your life and something you can forever be totally proud of.

The all-important check list

- Don't tell anyone.
- Make sure your calendar chart is ready for tomorrow.
- Make sure your spreadsheet is set up and ready to go.
- Make sure you have decided on your one big negative area of focus and created a talisman if you think it will help.
- Make sure you have your list of positive reasons to hand or at least ready to start compiling and adding to.
- Have you planned something to do tomorrow to take your mind off drink? What's up your sleeve just in case?
- Have you planned an activity? Are you going walking, running, swimming, cycling, using your Wii or its equivalent?
- Have you cancelled any meetings / get-togethers where drink would be available?

And now...

- Throw away (preferably smash) that favourite wine glass, pint mug or tankard. If it's an heirloom lock it away somewhere you can't get ready access to it.

- Instead of swallowing it, throw your last ever drink down the sink and watch it disappear. Imagine it being poison which has been slowly but surely destroying your liver, kidneys, brain and other organs, and ruining your life. Hate the rotten stuff as you swill it away.
- Go to bed early and sober, you don't want a hangover on your first day.

Well done!

The first day

At whatever time of day you are reading this, hopefully you are feeling enthused and not too stressed up. Don't let your mind wander and think about never having a drink again because you need to focus solely on today, and getting through today. This is a day you make history.

You are only a few hours into your new life but already your subconscious can be advising your body to get ready to become massively healthier, and you can help your subconscious fix on that message by repeating it to yourself over and over again. You can also tell your liver it can start to regenerate, your kidneys can have a good flush-through of all those impurities (you might want to drink lots of water at this stage – just to help), and you can tell your brain that far less cells are going to be lost every day from now on and that it needs to up a gear because you are going to live a lot lot longer from now on. (Oh and ignore anything you read or hear about alcohol not damaging the brain and even being good for it – what would you rather imagine is inside your head, a nice healthy fresh fruit or a shrunken pickled mush?)

If in doubt...

If you do wonder what you have begun, read one of my stories, or read your own if you have written any. If not, it is a good time to carry on compiling and then reading through your list of all the positive and the negative reasons for giving up drink forever. Concentrating on these will really help. And don't be tempted to stop and put the day off until tomorrow, otherwise tomorrow will never come, but you already know that.

If necessary take one day at a time. You can manage one day without drink surely, and regardless of what pressures provide you with an otherwise excuse. Then do another day tomorrow with the same attitude. Then the next day. So go on - you can do this!

And remember...

- Make sure your calendar chart is ready for you to proudly add a star tomorrow morning.
- Make sure your spreadsheet is ready to kick into action and start scoring your success.

But don't tell anyone yet!

You have already managed a few hours, so not long to go until you can count **ONE!**

TIPS...

Drink lots and lots of water

Take some exercise

Find a good book to immerse yourself in

Find some time to be all by yourself

Go to bed early

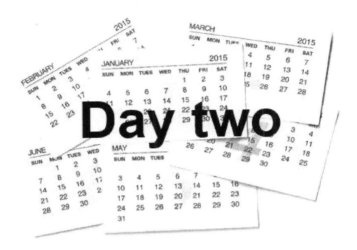

One whole day complete!

WOW, you can already be immensely proud of yourself. One day might not sound like much, especially if you didn't drink every day anyway or if you have tried giving up before, but this time it is definitely different. You have just completed one day of the rest of your new life!

How do you feel? I remember I was just pleased to get through that first day and I couldn't wait for it to be a month and a day so I knew for sure this was going to be forever. Not that I had any great doubts, I was just so keen to prove to myself I was strong enough and that there was no way I was going to fail.

As I am writing this by the way, I have just ticked off 600 days on my own spreadsheet.

I also remember drinking a lot of water on that first day, I was so eager to help my body flush through any vestiges of alcohol and to help my liver regenerate.

I created a mental picture of my liver and it wasn't a pretty site – all green and shrivelled but with one spot of healthy red from my one whole day of giving it a rest from drink. Every day I added to that mental picture with more and more healthy red displacing the green. I even began to feel sorry for it and what I had done to it and told it how it would be looked after from now on. If I would look after my liver it would look after me.

A lot of the gout problem I had was enhanced by becoming dehydrated. Not only does drinking alcohol get in the way of drinking plain old water, it actually dehydrates you thereby making the whole situation a lot worse. I now drink lots of water, probably three litres per day on top of the amount I have with tea, and especially with meals.

- Now is the time to stick a star on your calendar and if you have achieved anything else such as a swim or a run, mark that down as well.
- Initiate your spreadsheet with its first success.

It might also be a good time to think about writing a

blog or keeping a diary. The last thing you want is in six months to wish you had started a diary months before or from when you first became a non-drinker. You could write down how you feel even if it's to say you feel awful! Everything is worth recording at this stage just to have something to look back on. I went scuba diving off the beach by my house this afternoon, I really did.

My wife reminded me afterwards how a couple of years ago I used to watch the divers getting ready and how I would say I was probably too old to take it up again especially with my tendonitis and seemingly permanent limp. What a complete change; and when I came out of the cold water feeling invigorated and like a hero what I wanted more than anything was a really nice hot cup of tea. Alcohol couldn't have been further from my thoughts.

Swimming...

Most people know that swimming helps burn off calories, exercises most muscles in your body and helps maintain a healthy heart.

But just the act of swimming lengths gives you time to mentally unwind, de-stress and concentrate on the positive. Think of something you want to achieve, and whilst swimming determine how you are going to reach that goal. It is amazing how much mental energy you can focus whilst you work your body in the pool, especially as you become fitter and the exercise becomes a joy.

Day three

Two days complete - well done you!

All the alcohol has gone!

By now, regardless of what state you were in when you started or what size and shape you are, any trace of alcohol has completely left your bloodstream. That is the one upside of alcohol, once you stop taking it the body starts a clean-up process straight away. It is nice to know you could drive and be stopped by the police and happily blow into a breathalyser confident of it showing a negative result.

Some people say they get the shakes when they give up alcohol and worry it's because their body is in some sort of panic mode. You have to say calm and expect some sort of reaction, especially if you have been a really heavy drinker. Exercise is a great way of burning off any strange sensations you may feel, and of course drinking a lot of water to flush yourself through completely.

Yesterday I mentioned I drank a lot of water when I gave up alcohol, and I still do. What have you decided to drink instead? It is important to have something you can look forward to drinking.

I took up green tea as my replacement for wine and cider. For one thing it is refreshing; secondly you can drink gallons of it without any harmful effects, in fact it's good for you; and thirdly the act of making a cup of tea becomes a ritual to look forward to as a nice replacement for opening a bottle of wine. The one thing to watch out for however is that green tea is a diuretic so it might make you pee a lot. This only becomes a problem for me if I am commuting to work and there are no toilets on the train (I have a three hour journey most days), or if I am scuba diving in a dry suit like yesterday, and I want the suit to **remain** a dry suit!

I also bought in lots of interesting fizzy drinks such as cloudy lemonade, ginger beer and orangeade but soon found these sickly sweet and I preferred water instead. You will notice your taste buds quickly start to change.

On **my** day two I had unfortunately prearranged to meet some business colleagues in a wine bar in the City of London. I could easily have cancelled but I steeled myself to go through with it and ordered a lime and soda instead of my usual wine. I explained to my incredulous friends I had a rotten hangover to avoid unnecessary probing questions, but I found the lime and soda such an adequate substitute this has become my regular drink whenever I meet in a wine bar, which is now quite often. As well as being totally refreshing, lime and soda has the additional advantage of costing a fraction of the price of a bottle of wine, in fact some wine bars in the City don't even bother to charge anything!

By the way, a friend of mine took up drinking cola when he gave up alcohol but was on six pints of the stuff per day and ended up looking like Father Christmas. The latest 'Dr Who' described cola as being like the Tardis, it contains so much sugar it's bigger on the inside than the outside. My friend now drinks lime and soda instead.

That is three whole days complete.

Freedom

I thought it would be useful at this stage to insert a short chapter full of interesting situations all of which might make you wonder why you didn't give up drinking years ago.

Some of these relate to recent experiences of mine since I stopped drinking and some are reminders of other situations where drink really did get massively in the way of my enjoying life.

As I mentioned in the introduction to the book, I really have found a whole new sense of freedom since I ditched alcohol. You **will** experience exactly the same as soon as you relax and realise just what a huge change is taking place.

I suggested in my **methodology** section that you compile a list of similar situations you yourself experience over the coming weeks and months. This is certainly worth coming back to time and again as it is only after two years I have fully begun to appreciate just how dictated to by alcohol I had let myself become. And given that alcohol is not addictive it just shows how the thought of **wanting** a drink can worm its way into your mind and turn into the **need** for a drink, which of course you physically don't.

I believe alcohol addiction is a myth

It's all in the mind, you really truly don't need it!

Drink related scenarios and a new found Freedom

Freedom

I list here some drink related scenarios from a recent holiday to India where I have really enjoyed immense pleasure and a sense of pure freedom from no longer being a drinker. It will be interesting to see how soon your own experiences compare:-

- On the plane over to India we flew Jet Airways. I didn't see any free alcoholic drink being handed out but it was apparently for sale if you needed it. That would have proved embarrassing, calling the steward over every half hour on a nine hour flight to buy my next alcohol fix. In any event I arrived feeling fresh and ready for anything which was just as well as we went straight from Amritsar airport to the Golden Temple for a magical evening.

- I used to get incredibly dehydrated on the plane from all the alcohol consumed and swell up horribly. Sometimes it would take half the holiday to get back to normal.

- The service in all the hotels we stayed at was very slow. As I was only ever waiting for a pot of tea it didn't bother me in the least. Some of the others on the trip (there were 25 in all) were tearing their hair out for a beer.

- We made four train trips averaging seven hours each. There was no buffet car and alcohol is not allowed on Indian Railways. The old me would have been going spare!

- Most days we had a 4.30 a.m. start as we had so much territory to cover. The old me would have only got to bed at midnight and so still been drunk! Consequently I would probably have fallen fast asleep on the coach (and eventually woken up parched and feeling horrid) and missed sunrise over this magical land and seeing the country come alive for the new day.

- As part of the organised tour (and regular obligatory factory visits where the guides hope to get some commission from sales of over-priced genuine 'hand-made' goods) we visited a jewellers which was deathly boring (for me) but they did hand out a rum and coke for each of us on arrival – I had tea. As the visit lasted two hours that one alcoholic drink would have left me mad for more and no more was forthcoming. It was amusing to watch some of the other men on the trip squirm and stare longingly at the bottle of rum left tantalisingly open on the sales counter.

- Apart from in the hotels there didn't seem anywhere else to buy alcohol. The only solution for many of the others was to buy expensive drinks from the hotel to have in their room or go to the grotty bars in the hotels, most of which seemed to be playing loud local music and had TV's on every wall showing obscure cricket matches – thankfully I didn't need to go in any of them!

- At check-out time my bill averaged £1.50 for water. Most of the others had been boozing in their rooms all night and were handing over loads of cash, just like I used to.

- Despite the above, no-one drank anywhere near as much as I used to. I would have felt very awkward and very much the alcoholic in the room.

A few more horribly stress ridden scenarios I look back on and wonder why on Earth I didn't just give up drinking long ago. Recognise many of these situations?

- Cycling home from the train station in the cold and pouring rain wearing a business suit and balancing my laptop case on the handlebars, just to avoid drink driving and because I didn't want to suffer a business lunch without my compulsory few glasses of wine. I even remember once throwing the laptop case into a field I was so distraught, fed up and miserable! Why did I do it?

- Being given a ridiculously small glass of sherry at a dinner party, emptying it within seconds, and then realising everyone else's glass is still full and that I would have to wait ages for a top up even if that was likely to be forthcoming. How much stress do you need? Or do you want to stand out like Oliver Twist. 'Please Sir, can I have some more?'

- Drinking rotten tasting beer because that is all the pub had to offer and knowing it would give me a terrible headache the next day. Was it ever worth it?

- Being in a restaurant that only has awful wine on the menu but ordering a bottle anyway, hoping it will taste better by the third glass and then drinking the whole lot because it's there, despite knowing it would give me a terrible headache the next day.

- Being in a restaurant that only has either awful wine on the menu or very expensive wine and having the quandary of either ordering the rubbish wine knowing it would give me a terrible headache the next day or the expensive wine knowing everyone else on the table will want to help drink it for me!

- Having dinner at a restaurant with a crowd who say they don't want a drink and then decide they will have a glass of wine after all from your expensive bottle when you kindly offer it to be polite. Then when that only leaves you one glass for yourself and so you order another bottle, they either look at you as if you are an alcoholic or the b******* have a glass each of that bottle as well!

- Someone makes you a gin and tonic but you can't taste the gin!

- Someone buys you a gin and tonic but it's only a single measure and you know you need at least a double!

- Being at a dinner party where the host is stingy with drink and everyone is else is driving so they don't care!

- Being at a dinner party where you are the one driving so can only have two glasses at most – it would be far less stress to have nothing at all, and the party is going to go on until the small hours!

- Anywhere where the service is slow!

- Anywhere where the dinner is a buffet and despite your constant looking and searching for him to the detriment of enjoying your meal, the wine waiter doesn't come over to take your order until you have nearly finished the main course, and then you still have to wait for the drink to turn up!

- Getting home from an evening out where you were unable to have much to drink, so even though your partner has gone to bed because it's late you sit up and have another drink you don't really want, but just for the sake of it. Why?

Worst of all;

Going into work still feeling light headed and 'not all there' from the day before, and with massive internal stress knowing you were 'out of order' yesterday afternoon through too much drink and there are even things you might have done or said that you can't clearly remember. You know there is going to be some form of retribution at some stage today, especially as your work colleagues are avoiding making eye contact with you, the boss' door is closed and he is with someone from personnel, and the awful word 'sack' looms ever larger in your mind!

Freedom

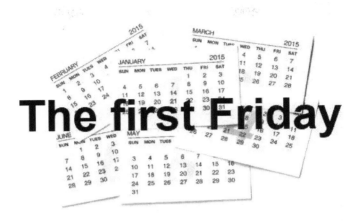

The first Friday

Today is a very big day. If you were just giving up drink for one month of the year like some of your friends might be doing or have done, it wouldn't be such a big deal because you could count down to when you can drink again. For you it's different. From now on every weekend will be one where you don't partake of alcohol and eventually don't even consider alcohol as part of your plan.

THINK ARMY

You need to be strong! This is where your willpower kicks in big time. Have a look at my chapter on willpower and remind yourself what I mean by my slogan – **Think Army!**

- Hopefully you have mapped out what you intend to do this weekend, and hopefully you are going to be kept busy and not be put in a position where you will be tempted with drink. If you are, well that's life – you just have to be very very strong. But write down what you **do** have planned, and tick things off as you achieve them. It all helps to focus.

- Now is the time to read through all the notes you have made. Reflect on all the reasons you now proudly don't drink and think about all the positive things in your life from now on. You might even want to rewrite them as a way of committing them to memory

- Keep your talisman in your pocket/handbag. Give it a good squeeze if you need to focus your mind away from temptation. Pour all the negative waves into the talisman, it really can help.

I remember just wanting to get that first weekend out of the way so I could relax and know in myself that I could do this no drinking thing. I knew that if I could do a whole week on the basis of never drinking again, I really could do forever. After all what is the point of giving up just for a week, only then to undo all the good you have done and go back to the life you have decided to give up?

Although I try in this book to look forever towards the future, you may be full of self-doubt at this stage and it may pay to reflect upon some of those more drunken weekends you have had in the past. That horrible feeling when you wake up with a splitting head, a giddy, sickly – not quite there sensation and that awful desire of just wanting the day to pass quickly so you can wake up the following day feeling a little more human. Or you might struggle awake desperately wanting it to be the afternoon so you can have another drink without feeling too guilty and hoping that a 'hair of the dog' drink will ease the pain in your head and the feeling of death inside.

What a rubbish way to live your life! How much better to always feel keen and alert and healthy, or at least if you are ill, knowing it has nothing to do with the poisons you have deliberately poured down your throat. I look back on those dreadful days and think what a waste they were, no matter how much fun I was having whilst getting drunk, it was never worth the horrible experience the day or even sometimes days after.

Drinking is only a bad habit

If it all gets too much, go for a long walk on your own (assuming you can), or at least be by yourself and tell yourself you don't want to be a drunk the rest of your life. You are going to make yourself so proud and achieve so much more. You are already clear of the drink having got this far so you know your body can cope without it. Alcohol is not like heroin or some other massively addictive substance, it is only habit that made you drink all the time.

- Have you told anyone yet? If not I would wait a while, at least until after the weekend when you can launch into week two knowing you have already achieved a small miracle for yourself.

- Think ahead. Think how fantastic you will feel going to bed on Sunday night knowing you have managed a whole week including a whole weekend with no drink. Imagine laying your head back on the pillow and feeling so wonderful, you might even sleep a whole lot better, I certainly did and have done ever since I gave up drink.

THINK ARMY

The first weekend

Yesterday we talked about planning for this first weekend and keeping yourself busy. It has certainly been a big week for you and you may just want to keep your head down, go for walks, get some exercise and get the weekend over as soon as you can so you can celebrate a whole week accomplished (assuming you started on a Monday) or at least getting over the first weekend hurdle.

If you have any time on your hands now would be a very good opportunity to sit and write a story of your own, or make some preliminary notes, draw that picture etc.

I have included one of my stories in the next few pages to provide you with some ideas, to provoke some thoughts on the whole subject of drinking, and to hopefully raise a smile.

The story is called 'Desert Island Syndrome' and I have deliberately chosen to include it at this stage just in case you are still finding it hard to imagine a life without booze. It takes me back to my teenage years when I first started drinking, I hope you enjoy it.

A story - Desert Island Syndrome

I am not sure what first sparked the thought process, it may have been listening to a radio advertisement for BBC's 'Desert Island Disks', or perhaps memories of watching the weekly and somewhat disturbing black and white TV programme 'Adventures of Robinson Crusoe' as a child, but I have often wondered what it would be like to be marooned on an island all by myself or preferably with a female companion. Most of these daydreams seemed to occur when I was a teenager laying on a beach or round the pool in some Mediterranean resort, after a few days of having soaked up some Sun so I had the semblance of a tan, still soaking in too much cheap alcohol from the night before, having given up on the boring but even cheaper novel I had been reading, and leering through heavy eyes at a pretty girl a few sun loungers distant.

My far away wonderings never wandered very far away however because two things always clouded the vision – cigarettes and booze.

I would imagine myself being slim and bronzed and looking every bit the complete hero, and the girl (being by myself never lasted more than a millisecond and the girl would be the leered at one I had my eye on at the hotel but was too shy to approach) would have fallen madly in love with me and be totally dependent on me for her safety and my prowess as a hunter and provider. Just like the castaway in the TV show, the boat that sank and left the two of us marooned would have been full of all sorts of essentials that would have conveniently washed ashore and be there to provide for all our everyday needs. There would be wood and sailcloth to make a nice secure fortress style home from (I would assume for myself innate carpentry expertise, and looking back I would have needed a wand or magic powers as I never thought to imagine any tools), fishing and scuba gear to help us find food (the fish would actively seek me out and want me to catch them), some Superman comic books to read when I wasn't busy chasing the girl round the island - who was all too easily caught, a gun with a limitless supply of ammunition just like the ones they have in the movies in case of attack from aggressive natives who might want to steal the girl, but in the event of their only being one or two aggressive natives I wouldn't need the gun being a Karate black belt already (In reality my martial arts experience was limited to just one Judo lesson when I was about six - I never went again because the bossy teacher lady had incredibly smelly feet, kept throwing me violently to the floor, and then pinning me down by placing a reeking foot on my neck), and ample supplies of toiletries, make-up and pretty clothes so the girl could stay looking beautiful.

I know - this comes across as very chauvinist but it is after all a teenage boy's daydream.

There would also be a record player of sorts that magically never ran out of power and came with an unlimited supply of fantastic music for every mood but especially reggae, Top of the Pops and even some Mantovani as I was into ballroom dancing big time (this was the 70's after all), and finally a grand piano (another innate skill!)

It goes without saying that there would be ample supplies of fresh water and fruit on the island, and that the weather would be sublime except for the occasional tropical storm which would not faze me but terrify the girl and make her rush into my arms. But by far the most important of all, the boat would have contained a huge supply of cigarettes (my brands - the one the big tough looking cowboy smokes sitting on his horse and the one picturing a 'ship of the desert' with, if you look closely, a boy urinating as one of its legs) and booze.

Now however much I fantasised about the other articles in my daydream, the only two items that actually caused any degree of stress were the cigarettes and the booze. I could actually imagine this castaway scenario happening for real and would conjure up all sorts of events that would cause me to end up with the girl on some remote island (plane crash, boat wreck, tidal wave before we started using the term tsunami), and in each case everything would turn out delightfully for the best. But whenever I came back to considering fags and booze the image would fade and the dream evaporate. Their continued supply was going to be an issue and I simply could not imagine living without either of these two essentials to human life.

Actually if I am strictly honest, the girl also had the potential to cause considerable stress but this was fortunately manageable. If after a few days of leering at her the girl so far lucky enough to be sharing my imaginary scenario had shown no obvious real-life interest in me (she hadn't taken the trouble to come and chat me up with a sort of 'you look really ever so nice, fancy a game of table-tennis big boy' type line) she would be mentally replaced in the following classic manner. On one of our regular promenades along the desert island fore-shore and obviously not holding hands we would discover strange but small and dainty footsteps in the sand, follow these to some previously unseen cave, and there find two small and dainty feet belonging to a beautiful, sexy and far more outgoing Girl Friday similarly lost and all alone. The two girls would naturally fight over me, the bitch 'I don't want to hold your hand' leered-at girl would lose, and then find herself dumped in no uncertain manner and left in the cave to wish she had been a little more forthcoming, whilst Friday and I pranced and skipped merrily away to carry on with the daydream.

(Look I know this is really sad, but I say again it is a teenage daydream, I haven't just thought it up, I promise. I'm not like that.)

But back to the essentials. Cigarettes would be considered first as they are easier to depict, coming in nice packages as they do. I would try and work out how many I would need to have with me to last let's say three years. Smoking at the rate of a packet of twenty a day (the girl never smoked as they would make her breath smell) that's about 1,000 packs or 100 cartons. That's a lot of cartons but within the realms of reason, and quite what happened after three years I can't remember ever deciding. We were probably rescued and the girl got traded in for a new moped, or perhaps some bigger than me Spanish b*****d woke me from my reverie by chatting up the leered at girl and walking off with her.

Booze was far more difficult to cope with, especially as the girl would need to drink as well so she wouldn't become unbearable and just nag endlessly on about being marooned with some bloody drunkard (*more alert readers will be able to tell that this bit of the daydream was added much later and with the experience gained from three marriages*), and to really enjoy ourselves we would additionally need a massive supply of mixers and ice, my favourite tipple at the time being gin and tonic. No, the booze was always going to run out pretty swiftly and make life on the island impossible, after all, what is the point of being in paradise if you can't spend the whole time pissed.

Now I'm a lot older I have actually been to a number of desert islands, not alone but with my wife and never marooned but as good as, most of these having been in fairly remote parts of the World. The most recent of these escapes was in the Bay of Bengal off the coast of Myanmar (Burma) last year, and having watched Tom Hank's *Castaway* on the flight over I was reminded of my teenage desert island scenario. I have to say that with the wisdom of my years, having had a very rewarding life so far, no longer being a drinker or a smoker, and having chosen the girl of my dreams to be marooned with me (I wouldn't last long with just my own company), I think I would cope very well indeed. I have even taken up karate and scuba diving just in case.

As a final thought on this strange subject, I recently re-read *Lost Horizon* written in the 1930's by James Hilton who also wrote the schoolboy favourite *Goodbye Mr. Chips*. It is the book in which he invents Shangri-La, the mystical hidden mountain paradise where as long as you are a white European, preferably English, and certainly not a local Tibetan (they have to do all the fetching and carrying and get paid a pittance) you live for hundreds of years, eventually lose all bodily desires, spend your time in thoughtful contemplation and find an inner wisdom and peace. Reading between the lines with my fresh non-drinker's eyes, it is interesting to note that for the first few years the new in-mates are allowed unrestricted access to the local Tibetan village, most especially its open all hours ale house where it would seem you get a free woman with every pint drawn, and are given a daily plug of much needed tobacco as they all love a good pipe. Even after many decades, when they have finally learnt to turn their back on these evil traits that keep us hidebound to our animal existence and have joined utopia, they still have a ready supply of narcotics to hand. Obviously in his unattainable vision for his Lost Horizon Mr. Hilton himself found it impossible to imagine life without those two essentials, fags and booze. But at least he left us with that wonderful word Shangri-la to captivate the imagination and spawn a great evocative song of that name by the Electric Light Orchestra. Perhaps after all those years of wonderings I have finally found a workable Lost Horizon for myself.

- **Would you like to be marooned on a desert island away from all the stresses of the modern world?**

- **Have you ever imagined yourself in such an environment where you are cut off from alcohol and or cigarettes?**

- **How do you think you would cope and what essentials would you need with you to help you survive?**

- **What is your ideal Shangri-la?**

- **Would you like to live for hundreds of years and what would you set out to achieve?**

Incidentally, if you haven't yet read James Hilton's *Lost Horizon* I thoroughly recommend it, it is thankfully very different from the Hollywood version of the tale with it's silly ending!

By the way:

Ever since I was a teenager I wished I had learnt karate as a kid, just to give me that extra confidence and inner power you get from knowing you can handle yourself in an awkward situation. I never seemed to have the time, I always had an excuse not to start learning and went to the pub instead. Now I go every Friday night. I'm already on my third belt, give it a few more years and I'll be a black belt!

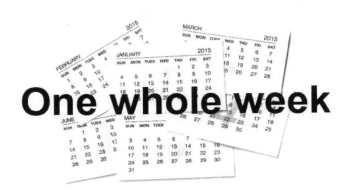

One whole week

What a fantastic achievement.

You can be really really proud of yourself, and your star chart and spreadsheet will be starting to fill up.

How do you feel? I know that even after just one week I felt like a new person. My eyes were clearer and brighter, I felt more alert and agile, I had far more energy – more get up and go, and I felt more positive about everything. Of course you might feel the complete opposite. It is obviously stressful giving up drink and if you have really struggled to get this far it could leave you feeling worn out. If that is the case just try and relax, you are over the worst and if you do feel like a wreck on the outside, just think how much cleaner and healthier you are on the inside!

Have you been exercising as well, as suggested? If so that should also be making a difference already. You might ache from using muscles that haven't been tested for years, you might even feel exhausted, but if so that is positive tiredness. It means your body has been working and getting better and fitter and healthier and getting rid of years of abuse and neglect.

Hopefully the weekdays ahead will seem like a breeze now you have managed a weekend, there should be little temptation to have a drink at all. Next weekend may already seem a bit daunting however.

I remember thinking just that. Thinking to myself that I have managed one weekend but I actually missed having a drink and relaxing with a glass of wine, or rewarding myself with a cider for having mowed the lawn, and consequently was not looking forward to the weekend ahead. But strangely enough when the second weekend finally came around I didn't want a drink after all. I didn't want to undo the good work I had done and have to start all over again having failed. I also made sure I had lots of activity planned to keep me busy. I also came clean with my wife that I had given up drink forever, and I enlisted her help to make sure I got through that second and all important weekend without being put in the way of temptation, and asking her to watch to make sure I didn't waver. I found that just telling her and seeing her positive reaction was all I needed as an incentive.

Have you told anyone yet? Now might be the time to let your partner or whoever is closest to you know, so you can enlist their support. Don't tell you pals yet though. They might not understand just how important a thing this is, they probably won't believe you anyway, they might even take bets on how long you will last out, and they may be just a little too jealous for their own good.

By the way, how much have you saved so far? I saved over £10.00 per day so after a week it was like finding £70.00 laying in the street. What could you spend that on and not feel guilty? For the first few weeks I actually took the cash out of the bank on a weekly basis in five pound notes so I could see the pile swiftly mount up. I couldn't believe how much I had been wasting on drink, and £10.00 per day was a conservative estimate.

By the way:

18 months no drinking for me and 6 months no smoking for my wife and we went to pick up a soft-top sports car. It is not new but it looks fantastic, it drives like a dream and it effectively cost nothing as it came in below the budget set by how much we have saved since we both gave up. What a fantastic incentive if ever one was necessary – what will we treat ourselves to next year?

The day after
One whole week

This week you will be feeling chuffed with yourself, especially if like me it is a really long time since you have gone so long without a drink. I think in all honesty it was probably the longest I had gone without a drink for over thirty years!

(I used to jokingly boast I had once managed thirteen years without a drink, and then when people started to say how amazed they were I explained it was because I started drinking at age fourteen! No-one was ever impressed with that joke.)

It is also the week when people might well tempt you to have just one glass.

'Wow, you managed a whole week', they might say. 'That proves you are not an alcoholic and can give up any time, so go on have a beer with me tonight and start again tomorrow.'

YOU KNOW THAT WON'T WORK FOR YOU!

Don't be tempted, because you **will** have more than one beer, you **will** convince yourself that having broken the chain you might as well start again next Monday and drink for the next few days, and you **will** probably not try and give up again for months.

You have achieved one whole week. That is a quarter of a month and a great achievement so ignore any negative waves and focus instead on:-

- Your new activities
- Exercise
- Spending the free time you have found usefully.

The latter might be helping out locally at a club or society by doing voluntary work. If you are able to work with children or vulnerable people that's wonderful because there is no way you can even consider having a drink and be looking after others.

You might want to read something educational or even do a course. There are hundreds of free internet based study courses leading to new skills and many of which come with a diploma at the end. Or you could do a paid-for course with a body like the UK Open University and gain a qualification as well as learning new skills and opening up new opportunities.

You could even decide to read that classic novel you have been putting off opening for years. I started reading Dickens and was truly amazed at how clever and funny his stories are. There is a wonderful drunken scene in David Copperfield that simply has to be read by anyone who used to be a drunk. Pickwick Papers is another of his novels bursting with hilarious drunkenness!

Is your star chart helping by the way? I found some old star charts of mine and have included a couple overleaf. The little ritual of adding that star every day really helped me to focus and stay on track.

My first star chart?

I recently came across the first adult star chart I created which dates from when I gave up smoking. I probably had loads of star charts when I was a young child, although if any were to acknowledge good behaviour there would have been plenty of empty spaces!

I started the no-smoking chart in 1992, and the fact that I still have it tucked away in my keepsake box says how important it was to me. Christmas of 1991 my eldest daughter had taken a photograph with her new Santa-delivered instamatic camera of me drunk and passed out asleep on her bed after Christmas lunch and with a cigarette still in my hand. I was so appalled to see myself looking the complete slob I vowed then and there to do something about it and to give up smoking and cut down on drinking from January the first. Somewhere my wife has that photograph to threaten me with should I ever go back to being 'Mr.Christmas!'

Just like this time around when I gave up drinking, I took up swimming as an activity to do when I knew I was going to be dying for a cigarette and to hopefully leave me exhausted and certainly not wanting to smoke afterwards.

Also like this time I decided to go 'cold turkey' and just give up with the ambition never to smoke again.

Looking back at that chart now it is interesting to note how well I got on:-

I gave up on January 2nd, I obviously found giving up on the 1st too much of a challenge.

I gave up drink as well but only managed Mondays to Fridays and after two weeks only managed Mondays through to Thursdays. After a few months even that fell away and I went back to drinking every day.

I did swim most days building up to a kilometre at a time and 2.5 kilometres every Saturday. I even started timing myself and within one month had halved the time it would take me, managing a kilometre of breaststroke in less than twenty-two minutes, a fast pace I have somehow been able to maintain ever since.

After one month my wife started putting 'P' next to each Saturday. After all these years we were trying to work out what these might have meant until my wife remembered it stood for Paralytic. Obviously I was celebrating each week of not smoking in too fine a style.

I have to conclude that for me, giving up drinking and smoking at the same time and without any aid other than willpower was a bridge too far, and in any event I wasn't trying to give up drink permanently back then, just cut down my intake and stop the everyday habit.

What did I achieve?

- Over the year I managed 364 days without a cigarette and have never smoked since. That is 22 years now!

- I went swimming 176 times and swam a total of 221 kilometres.
- I managed a total of 64 days without a drink.
- I was marked down as being paralytic 33 times.
- I saved in excess of £1,000 on cigarettes alone (and at 1992 prices!)

I only got majorly stressed once and that was on my 35th birthday when for some reason I scribbled over the star chart in big letters 'I AM NOT 35!', which was a bit silly because unless my parents had been lying to me all those years, I clearly was 35! Mid-life crisis a few years too early perhaps.

(My wife started using the same chart to help her give up chocolate, but only managed a total of 21 days – hee hee).

Incidentally I started smoking at age fourteen and by age sixteen was smoking twenty a day, a habit I kept up continuously until I gave up as per mentioned above. I never remember looking back and wishing I still smoked and I can't imaging for the life of me wanting a cigarette now, but there was a time when I couldn't imagine life without them - if you read the story Desert Island Syndrome this will become apparent. But so it will be with drink, there will come a time (like now in fact) when I won't be able to think why I ever drank at all!

Another revelation;

25 years ago, I had just taken delivery of a new company car, but I left it at home when I took my new girlfriend (current wife) out for a meal so as to not drink and drive. Only having had what seemed like a glass or two, I decided to show off and take the car for a very fast spin when we got back. I was breathalysed and lost my licence. Since then I rarely drove in the evening for obvious reasons. Now I am free to drive whenever I want!

I have just found another chart from 1990 which my wife set up as a countdown to my being able to drive that car again after having lost my licence for a year. That is certainly something that could never happen again. In fact this very morning the local police were stopping drivers randomly as part of an anti-drink drive campaign leading up to Christmas.

Two things struck me. Firstly I was a little upset they didn't select me to pull over as I would have enjoyed telling them it is two years since I had a drink, and secondly the lack of stress I know I would have felt on seeing the police cordon had I had a drink the previous night and knowing there would still be too much alcohol in my system.

Two whole weeks

What an amazing journey you are on, and I am assuming that it is two weekends you have managed to bypass without a drink as well. Your chart and spreadsheet will be looking impressive and like they really mean something by now. Only two more weeks to go and that will be one whole month. That is as much as most people ever achieve, and once past that hurdle you have beaten all those show-offs who do the 'Dry October' or whatever challenge so they can pretend they don't have a drink problem and spend the rest of the year binging to make up for all that alcohol they missed.

People will have noticed by now that you are not drinking. Has this been an issue? Hopefully some people will already be saying how impressed they are and how much better you are looking, and how much chirpier and happier.

Have you lost any weight yet? Or have you put some on? If you are taking more exercise as suggested you should really be starting to notice the difference. Doesn't it feel great!

Have you been out for a meal yet, or is that a hurdle you are trying to avoid. Have a look at my chapter on eating out, you will see I have also written a chapter on going to a wedding and even one on your first really boozy event where you will be the only one completely sober.

Don't look at websites or information sources that pretend to be helpful but that simply encourage drinking!

Some people may have said to you that alcohol is actually good for you. I even know doctors who will say that drinking in moderation can help you relax, deal with stressful situations and even lower your blood pressure. Even the UK's drinkaware website www.drinkaware.co.uk gives ambiguous advice and keeps falling back on the 'drink in moderation' safety net.

Don't believe or listen to any of this negative advice. You know why you have given up drink and you don't need to be given excuses for just that one little glass of red wine per day. It didn't work for you and it doesn't work for you. You can't drink in moderation which is why you are on this page of the book. What you can do is use all your fantastic willpower to give up completely which is also why you have got so far in this book.

You are half way through the first month. If you haven't done so, write down all the changes you have noticed already. There may be more than you realise.

Eating Out

Eating out can be a dilemma at first, even if the people you are with don't drink it can still be difficult and you may have avoided going out so far.

For one thing the menu probably contains a list of alcoholic beverages that in the past you might have studied long before you bothered to look at what food was on offer. It probably gives a selection of wines you would have enjoyed sampling, or a choice of beers, and may well advertise some special cocktail or drink of the month that makes your mouth water.

On the negative side all you can do is try to ignore all the enticing alcoholic beverages and select something non-alcoholic instead.

On the positive side you will start to relish the food far more than usual as your attention will not be being swayed by what you would have been drinking (sometimes I didn't really care what the food was like, I just washed it down with booze). Also, if the service is a bit slow it doesn't matter. Whilst the others are getting frustrated waiting for their drinks to arrive with their anxious expressions of 'I'm dying for a beer' or 'I really need a glass of wine', you don't care, all that stress of needing a drink in your hand to be able to relax has gone! I remember getting really irate, especially if I could see 'my' bottle of wine on the counter and the waiter pretending to be busy doing something else instead of bringing it straight over.

Also on the positive side, especially if someone else is paying, there is none of that awful stress of will there be enough to drink; will someone fill my glass if I empty it quickly; will it be embarrassing if I keep helping myself to more wine; will it be embarrassing if I order another bottle; will they think I'm an alcoholic if I want more than anyone else and keep asking for more; what if I encourage another bottle to be bought and then everyone else decides they will have another glass after all and all I get from the new bottle is half a glass which makes me even more stressed up than before aarrgghh!

So what do you drink at the restaurant?

Of course the choice is purely yours but I find having lots of water to hand a great help regardless of what else I have chosen. You can only drink just so much fruit juice or soda before it becomes boring, but water always quenches the thirst and helps you enjoy your food more without marring the flavour. I have even come to relish having a nice glass of refreshing water.

One thing I did try, especially when first going out for a curry after I had given up drink was 'non-alcoholic beer'. On close inspection however it appears there is no such thing as non-alcoholic beer, it is all just very low alcohol. Now whilst the amount of alcohol is so low you probably won't notice it and it is unlikely to make you want something stronger, it might make you feel a little guilty when you want to be able to say to someone 'no alcohol has passed my lips since ......', so I would rather give it a miss. If you do know of a truly non-alcoholic beer that is well worth trying please drop me a note on my website, but I probably won't try it anyway, I have started to enjoy the subtle flavours of the food far too much to spoil them in any way.

And when the free 'brandy or liquor on the house' is offered at the end of the meal – a nice pot of tea instead thank-you.

And remember, at the end of the meal your head will still be wonderfully clear, you won't wake up feeling like death and with a horrible taste in your mouth, the bill will be ridiculously small compared to what you are used to, and you will remember everything that occurred and more importantly, everything that was said, especially by you. You can even drive home and save the taxi fare!

Bon Appétit

Here is a good opportunity to introduce one of my stories which involves a meal, it is one that despite how hard I might try, I will unfortunately never forget...

A Story - The Ballroom Blitz

There is a girl called Peggy in the 1930's children's book 'Swallows and Amazons' who is a somewhat timid character playing very much a secondary role to her overbearing elder sister Ruth who for some strange reason prefers to be referred to as Nancy. If Ruth had been an elder brother with peculiar tendencies that might have made more sense. They also had a friend called Titty, but I run the risk of becoming distracted from my own story.

I hadn't read Arthur Ransome's masterpiece when I was five years old but despite this, there was a Peggy in my life although she was anything but timid and didn't play second fiddle to anyone. My Peggy's full name was Peggy Spencer, and she was the larger than life terrifying tyrant who glared menacingly at little boys through horn rimmed glasses and who ruled without question the ballroom dancing classes held at the local Royston Ballroom.

Scary Peggy and her mild mannered husband Frank had given ballroom dancing celebrity status in the early days of TV, and her formation dancing team became very much the mainstay of 'Come Dancing' on the BBC, now replaced by the global phenomena of 'Strictly Come Dancing'.

Once a week I would be made to put on a horrific velvet suit complete with bow tie and tightly pinching patent leather ballroom shoes and be frog-marched off to dance class where, being completely useless and not knowing my left from my right at that age, I would be made to stand on Peggy's shoes and whisked around the room so that at least I looked like I knew the dance steps and so would not bring shame on the rest of the class. As for the all-important and intimate ballroom 'hold' given its own essential paragraph in all good dance books, Peggy would instead force me into position by grasping my right arm in a vice-like grip and burying my face into the waist of her scratchy sequin gown so I couldn't see where I was going, her free arm meantime playing host to a cruel set of fingers that pinched and reddened my left ear as punishment for not having a clue what was going on. Mum and Dad adored the dancing and would twirl past grinning at my discomfort made obvious by the tears in my eyes, and they were really very good, winning all sorts of medals, and my brother Paul who was five years my senior was similarly enamoured. Perhaps I was just too young, or far too short to be dancing with an adult, or far too conscious of the likelihood of growing up with something akin to a vegetable stuck to the side of my head. I hated it.

You can imagine my reluctance therefore, when eleven years later my mother and with a knowing look suggested I go and give ballroom dancing another try as something to do because I was bored. I was at that time thoroughly bored with school, bored with where we lived as nothing exciting seemed to happen, bored with going up to the local pub every night and playing darts, especially bored with not having and never having had a proper girlfriend apart from the girl who came and babysat for my younger brother but who I didn't like, and frustratingly bored with the fact I was too young to own a moped or drive a car and therefore totally reliant on the boring and unreliable train and bus service. Oh, and I hated team games so there was no way I was going to join a boring cricket or tennis or football or rugby or anything else club. I was even bored with setting fire to things, a particularly bad habit I had picked up from Paul.

Consequently I approached the entrance to the Mecca Ballroom in the nearby large town (we had moved away from Peggy's sphere of influence), with a sense of foreboding and an inner knowledge that this was going to be a complete and utterly boring waste of time.

How wrong can a young man be! This spangle bedecked and seductively lit paradise of dance contained a complete spectrum of women and young girls, all beautifully and femininely frocked and made-up, and all dying to dance with a genuine male partner, me being the only member of my sex to have crossed the threshold of this private harem for many a week. Forget standing on the side-line and trying to remember some of the steps from all those years ago, I couldn't wait to grab someone pretty and start spinning!

If you have never had much chance of meeting girls (I went to an all boy's school and lacked a sister), there is nothing quite as wonderful as ballroom dancing classes. First of all there was the exquisitely lovely dancing teacher who for the first half hour used me as her demonstration dummy and consequently I relearnt the steps in rapid time whilst held in her tight embrace. Then the next hour was a sort of ladies excuse me where every few minutes I would find myself dancing with a new partner, each earnestly holding onto me as tight as they could to avoid being displaced by one of the many hopeful alternative partners hovering nearby. They even fought over me. I loved it.

By the next week I had recruited two initially dubious friends to accompany me. I did this on the basis that one of them had a car, and because it would be easier to encourage some of the girls to join us for drinks afterwards if there was a group of us, and the plan worked a treat. The ballroom became a goldmine for girlfriends, and we even had things organised to the extent that the young girl who ran the small bar at one end of the dance floor would hold out gin and tonics for us to sip by way of celebration as we happily waltzed or foxtrotted past on our orbits around the room with our enraptured partners.

After some two years of this delight, not only was I an accomplished dancer and extremely fit because of it (dancing has to be one of the best forms of exercise), I had had my pick of the young ladies as girlfriends, had had numerous crushes on the less sweaty of the mature Mrs. Robinson style contingent, and managed in the interim to pass my driving test first time and purloin the use of Mum's car. So apart from having just been expelled from school and being threatened with being additionally thrown out of home if I didn't immediately find a job, things were looking really great.

Then I met a young lady who was a whole three years older than me, but who thought how sophisticated I was because I could dance and had a car and drank gin, and so we started dating.

Incidentally, the Mecca Ballroom I attended was part of the Mecca group run by a certain Eric Morley who also ran Miss World with his wife Julia. At the time his two nephews were friends of my brother and I, one of whom was very very camp and was the person who in his velvet jacket with puff lace cuffs flamboyantly draped the sash round the winning Miss World contestant on TV, and the other who became a well-known radio DJ and used to entertain all the Miss World contestants at London's Penthouse Club whilst they were in the UK for this annual carnival, and many of which I consequently got to meet, which was nice - very nice. Becoming besotted with the high-life and enjoying the cachet of spending most evenings in the heart of the West End, the same club also became something of a second home for a while and helped me swiftly dispose of the small inheritance I had been left by a distant aunt, which was not so nice.

So here I was, supposedly very sophisticated, but so far only having met my new girlfriend's mother who I could already tell didn't approve of me, and having been invited to Christmas Day lunch at her home to meet the rest of the family, but most especially the angry looking, vertically challenged father with the comb-over.

I think Baldy disliked me on the spot for a number of reasons. For one thing I was very sure of myself (My own parents spent a lot of time travelling overseas at this stage so I was left very much to my own devices and hence had become quite independent); I had also been through a couple of years of horrible teenage yob stage where I had been alternately a skinhead (without the short hair), a greaser (without the long hair), a hippy (without the drugs but I did have an Afghan coat – sort of), and therefore felt I was very much a man of the World; it was also plainly obvious his daughter was quite taken with me, and me being younger than her he must have felt she was being either ridiculous or being duped; I was also far too gregarious, making a grand point of shaking the hands or slapping the shoulders of the other male guests and kissing on both cheeks and briefly squeezing the females present; I was taller than him, and having made a detour to a local hostelry beforehand for a couple of large gin and tonics to put me in a relaxed frame of mind for this encounter, I smelt of drink.

Now it turned out that for whatever reason, Baldy was convinced that young men and alcohol should never mix, and his own prematurely thinning on top creepy looking four-eyed son in the tweed jacket with leather patches on the cuffs and elbows, who must have been in his mid-twenties, was a walking example of a young man who had obviously been taught to shun all forms of 'exotic' entertainment and probably still had to wear boxing gloves to bed. He was what was called in those days, square. My gift to Baldy of a bottle of cheap wine (I assumed everyone gave everyone else wine in those days, just like my parents did) was therefore received with a look of shock as opposed to one of gratitude, as was my response of;

'I'll have a large glass of red', when asked by the mother what I would like to drink.

Some tortuous hours later, the main part of the meal

was over, my 'small' glass of red had been topped up only once despite having been drained dry within two minutes of it initially being handed me, and we were all ten or so of us sitting round in paper hats waiting for the Christmas pudding to be served. I had been sat in the centre of the table opposite the square brother, with the fawning girlfriend to my left and on my right side a most amicable uncle who had been surreptitiously trying to top my wine up when Baldy wasn't looking, but without success. As the flaming pudding was brought into the room, the uncle suggested the ladies should have a Cointreau and that us men should have a Cognac each. Not wanting to upset his main guest Baldy acquiesced to this request but of course omitted to provide a drink to either of his children or to me.

'Oh go on, give the boy a brandy' shouted the kind uncle, 'You mollycoddle these youngsters far too much, what chance have they got in life if you don't let them experience anything.'

And so as the pudding was spooned out and after a short but heated debate between the senior males, a nice crystal glass of warm cognac was very reluctantly placed on the table in front of me. The same table which to keep its pristine mahogany surface safe had draped upon it a nice white linen tablecloth, and which now held ten best china bowls of steaming pudding, a huge jug of custard, ten silver spoons, a ladle, ten crystal water glasses and matching water jug, seven or eight crystal wine glasses some of which were still fairly full, a couple of full ash trays including one in front of uncle with a smoking cigar resting on its lip, eight crystal liqueur glasses, a bottle of Cointreau and a decanter of cognac, and a Christmas centrepiece made from fir-cones, brightly burning red candles, ribbon and some sort of twig material sprayed silver that had been lovingly made by the mother but which belonged in a second-rate charity shop window although I don't think they had such things in those days.

I don't know how it happened, I suspect foul play on the part of the square who had been giving me evil looks throughout the meal, but giving a self-satisfied nod to the uncle as I raised my glass and grinning at Baldy as I subsequently drained it, I thumped the glass and my arm back heavily on the table only to find that in the few seconds it had taken to undertake that act, beneath the cloth the two leaves of this fine piece of antique furniture had somehow become separated.

Had I then had the scientific knowledge I have now I could have spent a millisecond reflecting upon the myriad forces at play, with the momentum of my hundred and forty pound mass then becoming a fulcrum and creating a counterbalance effect on each leaf of the table. As it was, all I remember was falling into the centre of the table and thence onwards towards the floor, hearing a rolling smashing sound build to a crescendo amidst the screams of anguish and cries of dismay, sensing myself being mummified in the tablecloth together with the entire contents of the table, and then lying in a stupor of misery wondering what on Earth was going to happen next as separate rivulets of red wine, water and spirits trickled into my hair and across my face, down the front of my shirt and on through the cloth to ruin the beige carpet beneath; a strong smell of burning hair confirming the pain induced impression I had of being on fire making the nightmare complete.

'I TOLD YOU HE WOULDN'T BE ABLE TO HOLD HIS DRINK!' was all I could hear being repeated over and over as I was doused whilst being helped to my feet, and then led away to the kitchen to be swiftly patched and cleaned up, have some molten wax removed from the rear of my head and then tactfully handed my coat before being thrust towards the back door.

I don't think I have ever quite come to terms with the embarrassment of that episode, and to this day have no idea what witty remark I would have made to the appalled family had I not found myself alone outside in the falling snow with the door being firmly slammed behind me. Certainly as far as girlfriends were concerned this one was as lost to me as I was for words. It was back to the ballroom for me!

One month - and counting

You have now reached that magic point where very few people you meet will ever surpass. You have managed a whole month without a drink and there is no turning back.

One of the most exciting things will be turning the calendar page on your star chart to the next month, and especially when you post the first star on the new month.

On the radio the other day the presenter I was listening to was saying how he had managed most of October being dry but that with only two days to go how much he was looking forward to sitting down with a large gin and tonic. What a shame he was unable to go further and give up forever, but then maybe that wasn't his aim in the first place. Perhaps he **can** drink on occasion and leave it at that; perhaps he doesn't have a drink problem and just wanted to lose some weight. It is a different story for you.

Every day from now on will take you further away from what others have achieved. Every day is another nail in the coffin for alcohol and another day in a growing success story which is you! You really can be so proud of yourself as others surely are by now. So now you really can tell people about your achievement. They will all probably know someone who has managed a dry January or February or whatever, but they are unlikely to know many people like you who have turned their back on alcohol forever and kept it up.

I know that for me the one month stage was a complete turning point for those very reasons. I was entering unknown territory for most people who drink and that was so exciting and rewarding.

Give it a day or so and then take stock of what you have achieved. Look at the lists you have hopefully been maintaining and take stock of the changes that have taken place. Have a look at my freedom list from day 4 and see how many of those situations now hold true for you. Have you been out for a meal yet? How did that go?

I waited until I had managed 50 days and then I put together a list of achievements for my children. We will come to that shortly but in the interim let's take some time to think about drinking and ask ourselves some questions.

Let's talk about drinking!

Now things are beginning to settle down, you are well and truly over the first major hurdle and you are beginning to put the past firmly behind you, it's probably a good time to get a few things out in the open. The topics I cover here are based on questions I have been asked when people want to talk to me about my not drinking. People who don't understand why I drank as much as I did seem fascinated with why I started drinking in the first place, they always want to know how much I drank, and always want to hear one or two horror stories. So let's go, but it pays to be able to look back with amusement.

When did I first start drinking?

Until I was about ten years old I had only ever tasted beer which I did for a dare, and I thought it was disgusting and like drinking wet stale bread. But I used to especially adore the sweet taste of two particular fizzy drinks, Cydrax which tasted of apples and to a lesser extent its sister product Peardrax which as you can probably guess tasted of pears. These non-alcoholic beverages were produced by a no longer trading company called Whiteways who also made very delicious and very alcoholic cider. I think being an 'apple ciderholic' must have been in my genes because I also used to love the taste of so-called 'cider lollies' marketed by a company called Criterion Ices belonging to the father of a friend of mine.

Unfortunately neither Cydrax nor Peardrax were easy to come by and when I was aged thirteen and we moved home my mother decided that the nearest readily available substitute was a drink called Woodpecker. This came in similar brown dumpy shaped bottles to Cydrax but with a nicer label depicting a pretty bird and consequently attractive to young children. Woodpecker also tasted and smelled pretty much the same as Cydrax but made you feel woozy and a little silly after drinking a bottle (sometimes you couldn't even stand up!) and it had the additional advantage of making you feel less inclined than usual to do your homework. It was perhaps the fact it was 3.8% proof that induced these effects. I am sure my mother was unaware of this however or else she wouldn't have encouraged my eight year old brother to drink it as well. The fact that the kindly man who ran the local off licence happily served either of us children probably helped to enforce her view that it was harmless. Even our dog Thunder became an avid fan, and many an afternoon on the way home from school I would find him sitting in the doorway of the off licence making a complete nuisance of himself by growling at anyone who tried to get into the shop and by refusing to move. He wasn't happy until I came along to buy some of his favourite tipple.

It was about the same age I started experimenting with smoking and I remember mum buying me a carton of duty free cigarettes on the plane over to a holiday in Spain, and my smoking them every afternoon in a Spanish bar opposite the hotel where we were staying. I would sit with the teenage boys who ran the bar conversing in a mixture of pigeon English and Spanish and drinking large glasses of local apple brandy. Somehow I used to manage it back to the hotel for evening dinner, but usually taking almost as many backwards as forward steps, and having to stop a few times along the way to throw up. What joy!

How much did I drink, and how much do you drink?

There are times when I have probably over-exaggerated how much I have had to drink to show off my capacity for alcohol, but this has always been with drinking pals. Mostly I have played the volume down even to myself and especially if I have been drinking alone at home.

(By the way, a lot of people say to me they never ever

drink by themselves at home as this is the sure sign of an alcoholic. I did, but this was because I enjoyed drinking and liked the taste of what I was drinking. I would never had drunk any old stuff just for the effect it gave, it was always to enjoy the moment. I just didn't know any better and had never experimented with not drinking and having something else instead. I am now far happier having a nice pot of green tea to hand and especially so as there is no limit to how much I can drink. I don't get to that 'Oh blast I've had too much and feel drunk and it's only two in the afternoon, now I've wrecked the day' stage. Do you know the feeling I mean?)

I have never really been one for spirits although I have probably tried everything available anywhere. I did used to like gin and tonic but I would be just as likely to order a beer.

The most spirit I had in one session was one memorable evening at a local squash club disco I attended with two pals of mine as we had heard there would be lots of girls there. I must have been about seventeen years of age because I was still a learner driver, one of my friends was the same age as me but couldn't drive at all and the other pal who was a year older and who had wealthy parents, had borrowed his father's car and had driven us there.

Whoever had told us about the girls was lying because there weren't any at all, but there were lots of very sexily attractive older women who made ideal substitutes and very willing dance partners as their boring husbands were too busy playing pool. All the frenetic dancing and hormone activity must have greatly increased our capacity for alcohol because at some point the barman called the three of us over and said he had been counting how many drinks we had had, and told us we were up to a total of thirty two measures each, and he smilingly held up three empty bottles of gin by way of proof.

I thank whichever angel was looking down on me from above in those days and the fact that the traffic back in the seventies was so much less than it is today, because I am ashamed to admit that somehow we managed to drive home. The pal with the car was unconscious and hence incapable of driving so we dumped him in the back, I was at the wheel and capable of doing the gears and steering but too blind drunk to see anything, and the pal who had no idea how to drive could see well enough but could only tell me to go left, right or straight on. In the end we never went faster than about two miles per hour, we hugged the kerb until we hit something which we would then drive round, and it took hours and hours to get back to the house where our unconscious friend lived, and where we left him asleep in the back of the now heavily dented wreck that had been his father's pride and joy.

For the next few years I mostly drank real ale and

developed a large beer belly I was inordinately proud of (as most beer bellied men seem to be) and could manage many pints per day although I was often sick but didn't let this put me off. I even worked in a country pub for a while which is a huge mistake if you like real ale, as I just got bigger and bigger and would have probably exploded at some point if I hadn't fallen out with the owner.

I suppose I finally settled into a drinking routine once I started working in the City of London and most of my lunches involved copious quantities of wine. That was in my late twenties and ever since then I have mostly drunk wine and a rediscovered love of cider as far as regular drinks go. That is certainly the case in the most recent years up until I stopped drinking.

My favourite cider was average strength supermarket brand cider available in three little bottles. The great advantage of these bottles is the size which allows you to convince yourself you are not drinking as much as you really are. Drinking one big three litre bottle in an evening doesn't look as shameful as seeing five and a bit empty pint bottles lined up. It looks even less if you have two of these bottles on the go at any one time and make sure there is always something left in both of them.

Sometimes I would only drink two litres of cider but then I would be having wine as well, and nearly always white wine although I did go through periods of wanting nothing other than rosé for some strange reason. All a matter of taste I think.

So totting all that up if you'll excuse the pun, I would say on average since I was thirty years of age, I drank two litres of cider and one and a half bottles of wine each day. In units that equates to about 26 units a day which is a whole week's worth for the average male. In calorie content terms it also equates to about eight burgers a day on top of my normal food intake so no wonder I have lost so much weight since giving up. Scaring isn't it? But at least I'm being honest!

- **Have you ever been really honest with yourself exactly how much you drink, or more to the point honest with your family, your friends or your doctor?**

I talk more about me and wine in the story 'The Ultimate Test' that comes after this chapter, but first:-

A horror story.

You have already come across my most embarrassing experience involving drink in the story 'The Ballroom Blitz'. My most awful experience was a couple of years earlier when I was fifteen.

At thirteen years of age I was run over crossing the road outside my house. It was on a dark winter's evening during the power cuts that were a regular feature in the 70's due to the coal miner's strikes, and consequently there were no street or house lights and the car that hit me apparently had no lights on either. I say apparently because the driver never stopped to discuss the fact and I was too busy being unconscious and bleeding horribly at the side of the road. The end result of this despite lots of time spent in hospital was that I had to have much of my jaw repaired and to wear false teeth for the rest of my life (I must have landed on my face). As I was still a growing adolescent the dental surgeons were unable to build a bridge for me and so I had to wear a large removable plate with seven front teeth on it.

As anyone who has had old fashioned braces or a teeth plate will know I had to remove the plate to eat comfortably and at bed-time and the whole thing became a complete nightmare for a young teenager desperately keen to start dating girls and who was paranoid that the plate would fall out if I did any kissing, especially if it involved tongues.

By the time I was fifteen I still wasn't having much luck with girls especially as the false teeth had made me somewhat introverted, and it didn't help that the teeth had become a bit lopsided as the plate was getting mangled from having been in and out of my mouth so many times.

One particular late summer evening a pal and I were invited to an eighteenth birthday party in the next village. I remember it being quite a sophisticated event with lots of heavy rock being played, pretty girls dressed in hippy style clothes and most of the boys either arriving on expensive looking motorbikes or having their own car. It was also a very large and posh house with the stern looking parents of the boy throwing the party confined to a back room for the evening whilst we pretended to be cool and sophisticated but in reality made as much mess as possible in the rest of the house.

Being the youngest at the party I tried my best to look and act grown up and like a true man of the world and made sure the girls could see me smoking (a complete necessity in my youth) and drinking a glass of whiskey nonchalantly like I had been doing it for years.

After some time the party had settled down into the 'sitting in armchairs with a girl on your knee, lots of kissing, listening to loud music and everyone trying to look as cool as possible phase'. I was still bereft of a female companion and standing alone by the drinks counter feeling foolish, when three giggling girls approached and their leader asked if I had ever had a Mickey Finn. Not having a clue what this was but assuming it was something the Americans had invented and of a dubious sexual nature, I of course shrugged to indicate 'probably' and blew smoke in her face, as you do. Not to be put off she then proceeded to concoct a mixture of all the spirits on the counter (including some crème de menthe), add some orange juice for effect and then in a loud voice challenge me to down the drink in one. With all eyes in the room now on me and everyone watching for me to fail I of course rose to the challenge.

All I remember after that was a spinning sensation, suddenly feeling ice cold and finding myself alone outside in the garden, being dreadfully sick, and then my pal making me stagger and crawl the three miles home over dew-soaked fields to try and sober me up, and my just wanting to curl up and die.

Late the next morning I went cautiously and shakily downstairs nursing a throbbing head and feeling like I had climbed out of a grave to face my bemused parents who had heard me crash my way into the house in the early hours. It was then I noticed my teeth were missing.

Frantically searching the bathroom to see if I had left them on a shelf or put them in my overnight glass, and looking in every pocket of my clothes and nook or cranny of my bedroom I came to the horrific conclusion that I had somehow lost them when I had thrown up at the party.

Later that day, with my grinning father parked outside in the car and watching from a distance I duly and timidly knocked at the door of the posh house which in the light of day looked even more grand and forbidding than it had the night before. Fulfilling my worst fears the door was opened by the stern and ferocious looking father.

Trying not to dribble and sound too pathetic without my 'teeth' in, I said something wimpish along the lines of:

'Please Sir, I might have been a little ill last night, would it be possible to have a look in your garden for my dentures?'

Taking me roughly by the arm, this angry man then proceeded to drag me around his property from pile of vomit to pile of vomit, each of which he bent my head violently towards and in a loud voice explained was mine as he and his wife had observed me in my sorry state from the kitchen window. Were they in the pile by the greenhouse door? No. What about by the neatly manicured rose bushes? No. In the pile left untouched in the centre of the newly mown lawn? No. On the back door step and all over the boot scraper? Thankfully no. In the middle of the pile that had ruined his vegetable patch, yes!

Needless to say it took many weeks for me to get over that horrific experience and I never went anywhere near that house again. Neither did I ever again try or have ever encouraged anyone else to try a Mickey Finn. And the horrible teeth never felt or tasted quite the same in my mouth again either!

A Story - The Ultimate Test

My favourite wines in the World are Dom Pérignon champagne which obviously comes from that region of France, and Buitenverwachting sauvignon blanc which comes from a charming wine farm in the old Constantia region of Cape Town in South Africa.

I fell in love with Dom P because at one time that is what my Mum and Dad would drink, in fact before my Dad lost all his money it is **all** my Mum would drink. In the early 1980's Dad worked in the City for a large insurance operation and was one of what became notoriously known as the 'gang of four', themselves mixed up in an alleged and never proven multi-million pound insurance scam with another individual nicknamed 'Goldfinger'. This was big news in the City at the time and blown out of all proportion by the tabloid press who still seem to hate success. One reporter in particular kept fuelling stories about the gang of four spending every morning sitting in their plush top floor Director's suite drinking Dom Pérignon from silver goblets. Well I for one can say for certain that having joined them for morning drinks on numerous occasions, never once did I espy any silver goblets, but despite this the Dom P tasted just as good from the lead crystal glass my father would hand me having first swizzled it with his gold swizzle stick, now a treasured possession of mine.

That was all a very long time ago and the only time I have had Dom P since was on the day I married my current and forever wife in 2009, and as I can't afford and no longer associate with anyone who chooses to regularly partake of such an expensive luxury, my resolve in resisting being tempted to have just one more sip has not been tested since. As far as the Buitenverwachting sauvignon blanc is concerned however, it is a different story.

I first came across this wonderful wine on a tour of wine farms in the Cape some fifteen years ago. There are about six really excellent wine farms in the

Constantia region of the Cape and all are located within a couple of miles of each other. They are also all equally generous in the number of types of wine they are happy to let you try and in the measures they serve of each. Buitenverwachting was the last of these wineries on our itinerary and so I must have been completely blotto by the time we arrived, but despite this I remembered there being something very unique and special about their sauvignon blanc and so we decided to return the next day.

The wine farm (*I do like the way they refuse to use the term vineyard in South Africa*) is in a beautiful setting surrounded by mountains with the main whitewashed buildings with their green wooden doors being of Cape Dutch style and dating back to the eighteenth century, and is a wonderful place to picnic under blue skies and in the warm African sunshine on well-manicured lawns in front of the long lines of vines heavy with delicious fruit.

The description of the sauvignon blanc is best left to the owners themselves who write on their website: 'The wine has a pale lemon yellow colour and a bouquet of green figs with hints of gooseberries and an intrusion of green peppers. The wine is dry, full bodied and has a long lingering finish.' Delicious.

Both my wife and I fell in love with that wine and ever since make a point of scanning the wine list for its name whenever we eat out, and so it won't come as a surprise to you that we decided to make a return visit to Buitenverwachting a key item on our new itinerary when we were in Cape Town more recently. What might surprise you however, is that the itinerary was put together well after I gave up alcohol.

We found the wine farm every bit as becoming as all those years before and even more popular to the extent that the award winning restaurant was fully booked throughout our time in the country which was a great shame. Nevertheless I sauntered into the well-remembered tasting room with its long wooden counter, racks of sparkling glasses and bottles of mouth-watering wine waiting to be tasted and approached the smiling and ever helpful staff......

Wine has mostly but not always been high on my agenda. I first got the taste for wine as a young boy acting as waiter at my parent's regular dinner parties when I would steal the occasional sip. Much later when I was fourteen I remember buying a home made beer making kit at the London 'Ideal Home' exhibition I had attended with two school friends, but the resultant frothy mess tasted disgusting and made the house smell like a toilet so Mum made me throw it away and bought me a home wine-making kit instead. This was far more of a success and I usually had a few gallons bubbling away in demijohns at any one time, and I even pretended I was a commercial vineyard and made some artistic posters for my bedroom although I was always and ever the only customer. Most of the wine I made was country wine made from nettles or dandelions or even tea, but as a treat mum would buy me the occasional can of grape juice in the local home brew shop. It was the resultant wine from just such a can that put me off wine for a couple of years, and has ever since left me especially cautious of red wine.

It was a boiling hot summer's day in 1972 and it being a Wednesday when you were supposed to play sport after school which of course I didn't, I got home in the early afternoon. Mum was out shopping and my little brother was playing with friends elsewhere so I decided to take a picnic up to the downs just up the road from our house. You could walk for miles on the downs and there were plenty of secret glades where you could sit and think, or simply lie back and watch the few cirrus clouds drift by high above and try and make sense of the shapes they made. For my picnic I had brought along a large bar of peppermint chocolate, a packet of ten menthol cigarettes and a bottle and a half of the above mentioned home-made red wine. Unfortunately I had forgotten to bring a glass so I had to drink straight from the bottle which is never a good idea with wine. Also unfortunately, the wine had only just finished fermenting and so was fizzy after having been carried for a mile or so and if I had been able to see it through the dark green bottle, there would have been lots of sediment floating in it. Even more unfortunately, I had not yet been instilled with the knowledge that wine dehydrates you, especially when sitting in ninety degree heat and in bright sunshine without a hat.

Half way through the packet of cigarettes, most of the chocolate and well into the second bottle I began to feel a little woozy and remember the world spinning around me. The next thing I knew it was dark, I was lying in a pool of vomit and sweat and I wanted to die. I tried to stand up only to fall down again and vomit some more and started to shake uncontrollably. The spinning had also started again regardless of what I tried to do to stop it and I realised I was in a seriously bad way. The night sky being cloud free it had also become quite cold and I was only wearing a thin and sweat soaked shirt, and it was perhaps the cold that actually saved me because it made me determined to get home at any cost. It must have taken me some three hours to finally reach the back door of the house and find the strength to tap feebly and hope mum would hear and so rescue me from my misery. The whole way I either crept along on all fours or just used my arms, dragging my legs behind me. I did have the wherewithal to scramble off the path into the vegetation if I heard anyone coming, but this was to avoid the shame of being discovered in such a despicable state. The few times I attempted to stand up all ended in failure, another bout of dry vomiting, an even faster spinning sensation and a fresh attack of the shakes. I even crawled across a main road in this condition but thankfully too late in the evening for there to be too many cars around. I know I ended up a complete wreck.

You might think that experience would put me off wine for life, especially as wine was not a popular tipple in those days. Most families might open a bottle at Christmas or for a special occasion and even the pubs only sold wine by the glass from bottles held upside down in a dispenser to keep it fresh, the contents expected to last at least a week before the bottle needing replacement. Even on the annual package holiday most families would make a bottle last a week and put their room number on the label by way of claim. But I don't give up anything easily, and I persevered.

I went through the obligatory German Liebfraumilch stage of drinking either Blue Nun or Black Tower wine because the bottles looked enticing, to drinking cheap Italian Soavé and Frascati because it was the seventies and that's what went well with a cheese fondu or cheese and pineapple sticks, to the very occasional bottle of French wine which no-one my age ever really enjoyed because unless it was hopelessly expensive no-one had a clue what to buy. New World wines didn't feature back then.

I also returned to making home-made wine twice, and both times with a vengeance. During the most recent spate I had fifteen gallons on the go at any one time which when you consider that I was the only person brave enough to partake of the finished product, is a prodigious amount of wine. On top of this I was buying and drinking a bottle of shop bought wine per day and all this in addition to what I was consuming at lunchtime in the City.

We started by using the copious amount of empty bottles I was amassing for path edging in our country garden and we were also considering building a bottle tower of sufficient height to stand up in and enjoy the light coming in through the different coloured glass. But in the end we ran out of storage room and I ferried the bottles to the local bottle bank in numerous car trips over the course of one morning and had such a 'smashing' time I had to tell curious people who lived near to the bank, and who had come out to see what all the tremendous commotion was about, that we had had a massive party at the weekend. That sound of smashing glass is something I will sadly miss - I always made sure the bottles broke and made as much noise as possible - perhaps it's a hangover from the enjoyment of the wonderful Aunt Sally stalls at school fetes when I was a little boy.

So here I am in 2014, standing at the tasting counter in Buitenverwachting and about to ask a bemused young lady if she will let me have a glass of the sauvignon blanc to sniff for old time's sake because I no longer drink. Despite her confusion as to what a teetotal is doing at a wine tasting, she does, and it smells wonderful. But for some even more wonderful reason it doesn't set me off to have even the tiniest sip. Instead my wife and I sit in the garden admiring the view and the tranquillity and enjoy a cake and some nice refreshing rooibos tea.

By the way, if the fact I could consider using wine bottles for building purposes suggests I was drinking a lot of wine, at an average of a bottle and a half at home per day that is some 550 bottles per year. That equates to:-

- 46 cases of wine, or
- 1 pallet of wine, or
- at 7.5 cm width per bottle standing upright, just over 40 metres of path edging. That is a lot of path edging!

46 cases is also about what you can comfortably fit in the average delivery van. The picture below shows one of the two similarly liveried delivery vans that belong to the local off licence where I live. I think it represents quite clearly how far we in the UK have come from the days of wine being a very occasional tipple!

Whenever I walk past this van now, parked under its equally alarming sign, the allusion to it being of a medical nature presents to me a somewhat disturbing mental image.

I picture my nice rose coloured freshly regenerated liver as the centrepiece of a large contraption, and resting above a clear glass container but beneath a large hopper, and my liver being forced to act as a filter for all that wine which I slowly pour bottle by bottle, case by case, in through an opening at the top in a seemingly everlasting torrent, the poor thing. If I picture the image long enough the liver goes green, then puce green, then it develops lumps and bumps and finally it explodes.

I am so lucky I stopped when I did.

It was around 50 days I sent my first progress report email to my daughters which I attach.

If you are reading ahead to this page, either before you start to not drink or just to see how things pan out once you have started you will see a huge number of changes I highlight in the email, all of which are individually fantastic in themselves.

If you have naturally reached this point in the book, you too will have discovered incredible changes in yourself. You **will** be feeling fitter and healthier. You **will** be more alert and alive to life. You **will** be far happier than you have been since ages back and hopefully those around you are similarly happier to be with you and to know you.

Create your own list of changes to email or Tweet to someone, post on Facebook, Pinterest or any other social media you use, or just to be a bit old fashioned and tell someone about.

Think also of the hidden changes taking place. Your liver is busy regenerating, your kidneys are nice and clean and that all important organ your brain is buzzing with health. Your heart has to be a whole lot fitter too!

Well done you!

Why give up drink?

I have just started my seventh week!

- My face is thinner and never bloated in the morning
- I have lost over half a stone in weight despite all the swimming I have been doing to put muscle on
- I have just bought three new smart pairs of trousers which fit a treat and I am now a 34 waist down from 36
- I feel even happier in myself than I ever did
- I never worry about what or when I will be drinking
- My blood pressure is more normal than it has ever been since my records began – recommended top average for someone at my age is 140/90, I am 127/78.

- My heart rate averages at 52, this is athlete status.
- I never have a hang-over and wake up massively alert
- My breath is fresher and I only ever have a nice taste in my mouth
- My taste buds work much better
- I never have gout and all that nightmare pain
- I can drive whenever I want and have booked some evening drives to see the stars on our holiday
- My liver will be regenerating, my kidneys having a good clean out and my brain losing far less cells than it is used to
- I am full of ideas for what to do with my life for the next 45 years, and there is very little I can't do.
- Incredibly, I have so far saved a big fat £560!!

You know it makes sense!

My first holiday

La Palma February 2013 – and not a bar in sight.

At around 50 days it's also probably a good time to think about one of those situations you might be dreading or have dreaded well before you hit 'start', and that is your first holiday as a non-drinker. Here is the story of my first vacation at 50 days into my own new regime.

Most overseas holidays for me have always started at the airport with a drink even before we get on the plane. No matter what time of day the flight is booked for, there is always an excuse to have a glass of bubbly to get you into the holiday mood. The flight itself is the next opportunity to drink which might be something small like a beer on a short haul or copious quantities of wine on a long haul flight. I would lose count of the number of little bottles I would go back and forth and collect from the galley once the main meal was over and most of the passengers were asleep or in a daze.

My first new style holiday was a two week break on the Canary island of La Palma. Not having a drink at the airport didn't bother me at all but I was twitchy with anticipation of getting stressed on the plane having to sit next to other passengers drinking. In fact that didn't bother me either, I felt unusually calm and relaxed and anyway I was too busy reading a new novel to notice. One thing I did notice however was the lady next to me getting irate and 'tutting' because the hostess was taking so long to get to our seats, and she was obviously desperate for a gin and tonic. How nice not to have any of that concern.

The hotel was comfortable although meals were a buffet style affair rather than waiter service. Normally this would have been a real pain because it's nice to have the wine on the table before you start to eat and I could see most people having to wait until at least their second course before anyone took their drinks order. It was also the sort of place that unless you got in early there would be nothing left as most of the guests were piling their plates high even if they intended to leave half the food untouched. A rushed meal with nothing to drink is not my idea of a relaxing holiday dinner, but as water was already on each table and that was all we were drinking my wife and I didn't care less.

It was a bit of a strange hotel I have to admit as they catered mostly for Germans (keen on their beer the Germans), and so playing the theme music to Schindler's List every morning at breakfast time wasn't in the best taste in my view.

I think I'm also lucky that all the holidays I go on are either fairly intense as far as seeing local culture and day trips are concerned or like this one, busy days spent walking countless miles through the countryside with the occasional dip in the sea to cool down. I don't think I would have been able to cope with a 'do nothing but sit around a pool watching people get smashed fortnight', but then I gave those sort of holidays up when I was in my twenties.

We did have some spare time in the afternoons however, which we spent round the hotel pool and I bought a few cans of 'no alcohol' beer to try from the local shop as the hotel didn't have anything like that on offer. It was so gaseous and tasteless I gave the idea up after just one can and left the rest in the mini-bar as a treat for the chambermaid.

In the evenings before bed we sat on the terrace

enjoying the warmth and the tropical aromas, listening to the crickets and looking up at the stars. The Germans would be there with their pints of lager and shouting rather than talking, no doubt discussing the morning's music or competing with the crickets, or even planning which seats round the pool to bag with their towels that night, and my wife would order a nice looking (and nice smelling) cocktail. I steadily worked my own way through the menu of non-alcoholic cocktails but only one per night as how much flavoured juice can you drink without feeling sick. On the whole I found it very pleasant not getting drunk for a change and even as early as the first evening knew I would have no problem enjoying the whole holiday without being tempted to have an alcoholic drink.

One very big difference I did find on that holiday and others I have had since is that I was up and raring to go bright and early in the morning. We would go for a long walk first thing, sometimes even catching the sunrise and watching the village come to life, and return to the hotel to hide some of the German's towels and have a swim before a late breakfast and in time to watch our Teutonic friends react to their compulsory dose of Schindler. A couple of them even had a beer at breakfast time which is something I never would have done, and from the look of these unfortunates it was clearly to try and stave off a horrid hangover.

In summary then, I don't think you need worry about how you are going to cope with holidays without drink. Instead, go with the mind-set that there is so much more to a holiday than being in a bar and getting wrecked; so much more to see and experience, and because of it if you think about it, a much longer life full of far more holidays for you to enjoy!

By the way:

In the swimming pool on a holiday ten years ago, I picked up an infection in my finger nails which refused to go and my nails always looked crap and kept breaking. Since giving up drink, the infection has gone, my nails look normal once again and are nice and strong!

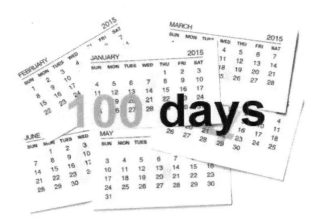

Does it feel possible – one hundred days! Did you ever think you would get this far? I think I knew after a couple of weeks I would be able to give up forever but I never really anticipated what it would feel like at various milestones. One hundred days is over three months or a quarter of a year, but then you know that.

A massive amount can happen in a hundred days. The most famous hundred days has to belong to Napoleon Bonaparte after whom the brandy is named although it is unlikely he ever tasted any preferring heavily watered down wine at most. In one hundred days he escaped from his island prison of Elba, retook the throne of France, consolidated his empire, terrified the life out of most of the rest of Europe, fought and won numerous major battles, finally lost his greatest battle at Waterloo when everyone else ganged up against him, and was shipped off to be poisoned in St. Helena (or so the rumour goes).

It was at about my own hundredth day that I bumped into a friend of mine I hadn't seen for a couple of years. He told me he had given up drinking for a year but then stupidly started again at a wedding and was back where he started from. He sorely wished he had stayed off the drink and although he wasn't drinking that much compared to what he used to, having met me he was thinking of going sober again. I think having failed once however and hating himself for it he was scared of going through the whole process and all that potential disappointment again.

Chatting to him really helped me in my resolve never to let anything get in my way of not drinking, there was to be no occasion so important that it would get me to have even one tiny sip of alcohol. I even considered (and this is serious) that if I contracted a life terminating illness and was given just three months to live, even that wouldn't get me to think 'sod it' and go and have some booze. After all, if you only had a short time left surely you would want to spend it with your loved ones and treasuring every single second, not being drunk and forgetting everything or daring to miss anything. At the complete other end of the scale I thought about winning millions on the lottery. Would this make me want to celebrate with an expensive bottle of Dom Pérignon? The answer once again was no, why shorten my life and go back to all that misery I have escaped from just because I am crazily wealthy. Rather enjoy the money in new ways and as part of my new life, after all, it wasn't because of money that I gave up drink, it was to change me for the better.

- **Would you go back to drinking if you won pots of money?**
- **Would you go back to drinking if you were given a limited time to live?**

As it happened I had two events looming where drink would potentially be a great temptation, St George's Day and my youngest daughter's wedding. Let's first see how I coped with the drunken chaos that in England is known as St. George's Day.

St. George's Day

Every year the English celebrate St. George's day and I am fortunate enough to be invited by a very great friend of mine to a spectacular luncheon organised by the St. George's Day Club in London. The event is actually held in a colossal Mayfair hotel dining room as there are usually some two thousand guests present, mostly male, and all hell bent on drinking as much as possible.

The first three times I was invited I was similarly hell bent. The day would start late morning at a pub nearby where the hard core members of the club would congregate. Spilling onto the road and generally being a nuisance to traffic and pedestrians, these smartly suited brethren wearing an array of military, club and sporting ties together with a large rose in their lapel, would tank up in advance of continuing on to the lunch itself. My friends and I would drink Guinness although after two pints of this very filling liquid I would prefer to move on to cider. We would always make a point of ordering about three pints each at a time because it took so long to get served despite the pub putting loads of extra staff on for the day, such was the demand.

Feeling suitably 'warmed up' we would then head en masse to the hotel and find our table which would already have as its centrepiece a huge ice bucket full of bottles of white wine and a similar number of red bottles standing sentinel nearby.

After grace had been given by some eminent gentleman of the church, white wine would always accompany the first course after which the 'roast beef of old England' would be piped in to the room. This massive side of cow would be welcomed with rapturous applause and eager expectation by most in the room. Not eating beef even in the days I did eat meat, I would instead look forward to the Yorkshire pudding and mash potato and hope these staple foods would help to absorb some of the alcohol that would by now be having a considerable effect on me.

Obviously glass after glass of red wine would be served with the main course following which the pudding would be eaten with a mixture of whatever drink could be found amongst the now myriad empty and half empty bottles littering the table. At this stage there would be a constant stream of men making their way to and from the toilets or simply circulating the room hoping to spot a celebrity sports star or someone off the television.

It would then be time for brandy and the many speeches but by this stage I would more than likely have fallen asleep at the table. On one occasion I was so blotto my table companions wedged me upright in my chair, put Union Jack flags sticking out of my collar and a serviette on my head making me look like some kind of waxwork dummy and took some photographs to taunt me with later on.

At the close of the event we would somehow stagger back to the same pub again for more Guinness and I would eventually find my way home many hours later, and swear to myself the next morning I would never drink again, or at least never mix my drinks.

When my invitation arrived the first year following my having given up drink I was naturally cautious of accepting, and made sure my good friend realised I would love to attend but that I would not be swayed in my determination not to drink.

When the day arrived I duly met everyone at the pub as usual and enjoyed being useful by helping to get the drinks and talking to other people similarly queuing to get served at the bar, and not being desperate for a drink myself found that experience completely stress free. Over the lunch I drank water but out of a wine glass so no-one else on the table even noticed for quite some time, and when the fact I was not drinking at such a drunken event became widely known, it became a talking point and a subject of wonder and considerable interest. Everyone was most impressed, wished me well and I felt very proud of what I was doing.

For once I was still awake to enjoy the speeches, and the waiter looking after our table and pouring the brandies managed to find me a large pot of green tea. He was very sociable possibly because apart from him and the other staff I was perhaps the only sober person in the room. I didn't join the others at the pub afterwards because by then they were too far gone to notice me not being there anyway, and I got home at a reasonable hour feeling still alive, having enjoyed a very grand event, remembering everything that had happened and without any nightmare photographs to haunt me for the next few weeks.

It can be done!

There is no particular reason for having a 250 day page, it just happens to be when I sent my second email list of achievements to my daughters and which I attach next. I remember suddenly feeling like celebrating and sharing the news.

Have you written to anyone to share what is happening to you? I hope you have.

What about a holiday? How did it go? I would to hear about your experiences so please do post something on my blog. If you do look at my website you will see I regularly post updates. These include things happening to me of relevance but also links to things I spot in the news that mention drink. There is an ever increasing focus on getting people to cut down their alcohol intake. The government always seems to fall short of telling people to ban it completely however, and I still notice that most talk always includes that get out line of 'the odd drink won't harm you and could even do you some good.' What rubbish, but then by now you will be thinking the exact same thing as me and will know the truth.

Why give up alcohol? The list just gets bigger!

I have done over 250 days

- I have lost nearly two stone in weight despite all the swimming I have been doing to put muscle on and have settled at 12 stone 9 pounds
- I am now a 32/33 waist down from 36, and most 34 waist trousers are too large!
- I feel far far happier in myself than I ever did
- I never worry about what or when I will be drinking – it no longer dictates any timescales during my day
- My blood pressure is more normal than it has ever been since my records began – recommended top average for someone at my age is 140/90, I am 116/70.**I have now been told to come off medication altogether, after 10 years!!**
- My heart rate averages at 52, this is athlete status.

- **My type two diabetes has gone away and my cholesterol is normal**
- I never have a hang-over and wake up massively alert
- I look great and consequently feel fantastic because of it
- My breath is fresher and I only ever have a nice taste in my mouth
- My taste buds work much better and I love being a pescetarian
- I never have gout and all that nightmare pain and am fitter than I have been for years
- I can drive whenever I want
- I have retaken up ballroom dancing
- I have taken up karate
- I have started scuba diving in the UK
- My liver will be regenerating, my kidneys having a good clean out and my brain losing far less cells than it is used to
- My psoriasis has vanished!
- My fingernails have cleared up and look normal.
- I go to the loo as I should be going!
- I am full of ideas for what to do with my life for the next 45 years; there is very little I can't do.
- **Incredibly, I have so far saved well over a big fat £2500!!**

You know it makes sense

You have now achieved the seemingly impossible and gone for a whole year without alcohol. I know how excited I felt as I approached and then made it to that magic one year milestone. It is such a fantastic thing to say to people that you have given up drink for a year.

Hopefully you have bought yourself a new calendar to carry on with a new star chart and have set up a new spreadsheet. I did and I still keep them both going every year. It was great fun totalling up all the other things I achieved as well, such as the total distance swum, the amount of times I went kayaking, number of karate lessons I had and so on. I also totalled the amount of money saved which was incredible especially as I know this was a very conservative estimate.

So how do you feel about carrying on? I have a friend who gave up at one year (I mentioned him at 100 days in this book) and that was all due to having a drink at a wedding. As promised I include my own story about a wedding next. That was my youngest daughter's wedding and I had to make a speech so the temptation to have a drink could have been huge, but it wasn't and I didn't. Make sure you don't fall into a trap and have just the one glass.

You will find as the next few weeks and months progress not drinking becomes second nature. You won't even think about drink except to constantly celebrate the fact you don't drink every time a situation crops up where being a drinker would have given you some sort of grief or would have been an annoyance.

Those around you will be celebrating your first year complete with you, and being so happy for you and because of you. Isn't this just the most fantastic thing you ever did?

Do keep your talisman handy however, or at least a mental version of it tucked away somewhere in your subconscious, you never know when you might relax your vigilance and be tempted to have just that one glass. Having something to focus on and that **will** remind you of why you don't drink really will help. If you haven't already done so, you might want to listen to the self-hypnosis session that came with this book, or listen to it again to reinforce the experience.

The wedding

You might have been to a wedding in the past few months, if you did and you were a guest it is relatively easy to have a soft drink or water, to keep a low profile and to leave early if everyone gets too drunk and you feel a bit out of place.

It's a little different if you are the father of the bride, you are expected to make a speech and toast the happy couple, you have to be one of the last to leave, and if the venue for both the ceremony and the reception is a beautifully situated wine farm in Franschhoek, about 50 miles outside Cape Town, South Africa!

The wedding was due to take place at 3.00 p.m. in the cellar used for wine tasting and proceeded by an actual tasting as a bonus for the guests before the happy couple made their entrance.

Not wanting to sit through or partake in the tasting, my wife and I instead stayed above ground enjoying the beautiful African autumn sunshine and talking to my new South African son-in-law to be. As soon as we caught sight of my daughter arriving however, it was time to take our places down below with the rest of the wedding party.

The wine tasting at this establishment is supervised by the owner of the wine farm, an elderly gentleman whose main party piece after his lengthy rambling speech about his German ancestry, is to take the top off a wine bottle with a sabre. Unfortunately, either he had already supervised a number of other tastings that morning or age had got to him, because he was clearly drunk, very drunk. Instead of finishing his show and then standing aside whilst a local hired dignitary masterminded the marriage service and introduced the waiting wedding couple, the drunken old fool kept mumbling on about his family history, waving his sabre dangerously around and generally being pissed as a fart. When he finally spotted my daughter standing looking frustrated and waiting to be married, he then mistook her for a further volunteer to help in his bottle slicing act, and started on his entire repartee again, even to the extent he put his drunken arms around her and tried to kiss his 'beautiful assistant'. I think if I had still been a drinker I would either have said something loud or thrown the idiot off the stage. As it was I merely felt how glad I was that for me the days of being a drunken fool are over, and waited patiently at the rear of the room. Thankfully some of his staff eventually braved being fired and dragged him away mid act to delight another party of people waiting upstairs. So far so good.

At the reception the food was excellent and the wine smelt very nice but I stuck to water as planned. Then when it was time for the toasts and my speech, my daughter had thoughtfully organised some really pleasant sparkling grape juice for me instead of champagne, and acting as if this was the real stuff and given the excitement of the moment I actually didn't notice the difference. After that whilst most of the others got merry, and in between short breaks to talk to people out in the late afternoon sunshine, my wife and I danced for hour after hour to the very good disco, and had a fantastic time.

Even more wonderful than being sober was not even wanting a drink. I think if I had been a drinker and had had to go without a drink at the wedding it would have been torment, but now 'I don't drink' it was just so easy and natural. I even had the additional advantage of a very pleasant late evening drive taking the beautiful coastal route back to our hotel in Cape

Town.

Finally, when I recently went through the wedding pictures to find a couple to include with this story, just looking at the eyes of the other people in the photographs taken later in the day, everyone except my wife and I and two little children look completely sloshed!

Why give up alcohol? The list just gets even bigger!

I have done 575 days

- My weight has settled at 12 stone 9 pounds – perfect for my height and build.
- I am now a trim 32/33 waist!
- I feel far far far happier in myself than I ever did.
- I never worry about what or when I will be drinking – it no longer ever dictates any timescales during my day.
- My blood pressure is below the upper limit for a male of 140/90 and that is without any medication at all.
- My heart rate averages less than 52, this is athlete status.
- **My type two diabetes has gone away and my cholesterol is normal.**
- I have so much stamina and I swim, walk and cycle every day. Most days weather permitting I kayak as well.

- I look slim and consequently feel fantastic because of it.
- People I meet keep saying how healthy I look, people I have not met for some time can't believe the difference.
- My taste buds work much better and I can eat anything I want including lots of puddings and sweet stuff and never put a pound on in weight.
- I never have gout and all that nightmare pain and am fitter than I have ever been in my life!
- I can drive whenever I want, and take Lolly for long evening drives to enjoy the sunset or the night sky.
- I have taken up karate, I am already a red belt and soon to be a yellow belt.
- I have started scuba diving in the UK and just got my dry suit diver certificate so I can dive in the winter or even under ice! My air also lasts much longer than it used to.
- My liver will have regenerated, my kidneys had a good clean out and my brain losing far less cells than it ever used to.
- My psoriasis has vanished, my fingernails have cleared up and look normal.
- My eyes are brighter.
- I go to the loo as I should be going!
- I am full of ideas for what to do with my life for the next 45 years, there is very little I can't do.

- Compared to what I was like I feel as if I'm in my early forties not late fifties!
- I am so laid back despite being so busy doing and planning things.
- I have published my first book and am writing four others including one called 'I don't Drink!'
- **Incredibly, I have so far saved well over a big fat £6000!! Although I have spent it on a lovely sports car to take Lolly out in!**
- Giving up has encouraged Lolly to give up smoking. She has so far done 260 days and as well as being massively fitter has added countless years to her life with me.

You know it makes sense

I haven't numbered this day page because you could be looking at this at any time.

If you have worked your way steadily to this point in the book you don't need me anymore. You have created your very own never-ending story. I don't need to say well done or how proud you can be of yourself because you already know that and countless others will have said the same to you.

If you have sneak-peeked to the end to see what happens, then I hope you can imagine the feeling of joy, liberation and wonder that awaits you when you work your way through to here too.

I really would welcome your feedback because the more people we can help to say 'I don't drink', the better a World it will be we live in. But then you know that too!

www.idontdrink.net

Thank-you for taking this journey with me.

God Bless

Your FREE self-hypnosis track

Dan Jones of the Sussex Hypnotherapy Centre has specifically created a self-hypnosis session to accompany this book. Even after two years of not drinking, I listened to the track whilst compiling this joint package with Dan and it really does help to cement in place everything I included in my methodology. It is a highly valuable tool and worth exploring at any chapter you are reading in this book, but especially within the first month of hitting 'start'. I hope you enjoy using it, and I would like to express my sincere thanks to Dan Jones for making it available to my readers.

Your free copy can be downloaded from my website by following this special link:-

www.idontdrink.net/danjones

Copyright

18922216R00136

Printed in Great Britain
by Amazon